AF538406

Through the Lens

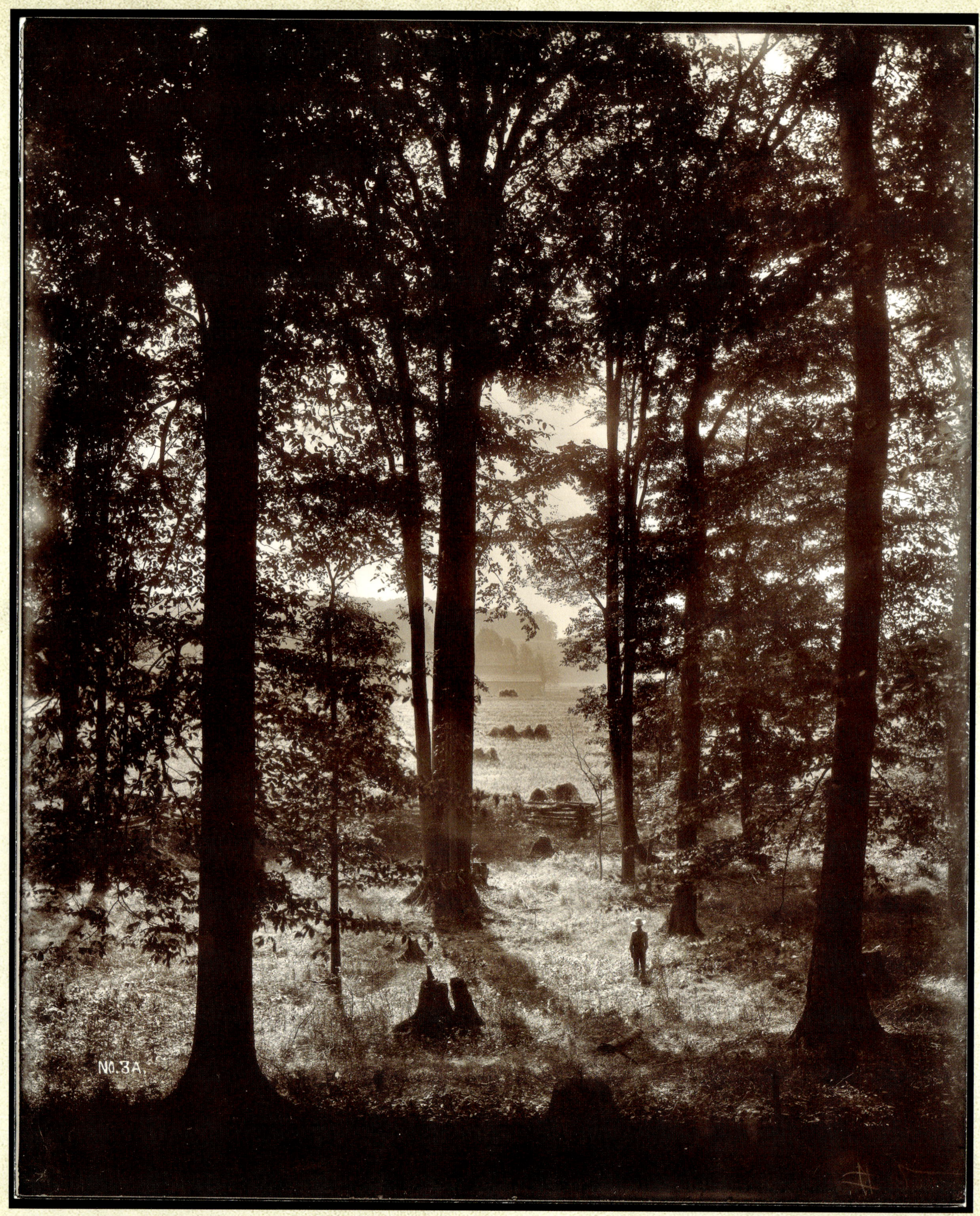

The Sacred Grove, Manchester, New York, August 13, 1907, Anderson Collection, LDS Church History Library, Salt Lake City, Utah.

Through the Lens

The Original 1907 Church History Photographs of George Edward Anderson

Andrew H. Hedges
Richard Neitzel Holzapfel

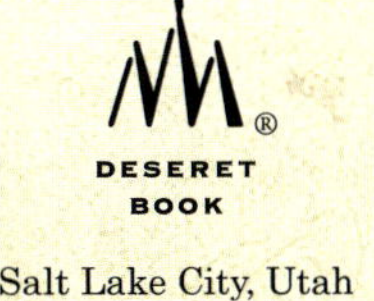

Salt Lake City, Utah

© 2010 Andrew H. Hedges and Richard Neitzel Holzapfel

All rights reserved. No part of this book may be reproduced in any form or by any means without permission in writing from the publisher, Deseret Book Company, P. O. Box 30178, Salt Lake City, Utah 84130. This work is not an official publication of The Church of Jesus Christ of Latter-day Saints. The views expressed herein are the responsibility of the authors and do not necessarily represent the position of the Church or of Deseret Book Company.

Deseret Book is a registered trademark of Deseret Book Company.

Visit us at DeseretBook.com

Library of Congress Cataloging-in-Publication Data

Hedges, Andrew H., 1966–
Through the lens : the original 1907 church history photographs of George Edward Anderson / Andrew H. Hedges and Richard Neitzel Holzapfel.
p. cm.
Includes bibliographical references and index.
ISBN 978-1-60641-236-7 (hardbound : alk. paper)
1. The Church of Jesus Christ of Latter-day Saints—History—Pictorial works. 2. Mormon Church—History—Pictorial works. 3. Anderson, George Edward, 1860–1928. 4. Photographers—Utah. 5. Photography—United States. I. Holzapfel, Richard Neitzel. II. Telford, John, 1944– III. Anderson, George Edward, 1860–1928. IV. Title.
BX8611.H43 2010
289.3'7309041—dc22 2010011477

Printed in the United States of America
Worzalla Publishing Co., Stevens Point, WI

10 9 8 7 6 5 4 3 2 1

To JoAnn, Hannah, Ward, Addison, Daniel, and Sam, my six superlatives

—Andrew H. Hedges

For my father, Robert William Holzapfel

—Richard Neitzel Holzapfel

Contents

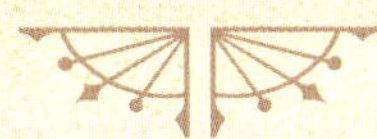

Photographs

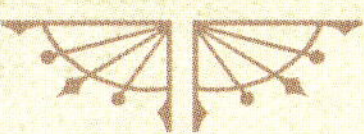

Prologue

George Edward Anderson's Photography

New England

New York and Pennsylvania

Ohio

Missouri

Illinois

Acknowledgments

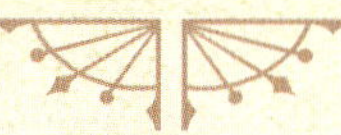

Many of George Edward Anderson's photographic glass plates of Church history sites have survived the ravages of time, and they are among the important sources we used in this project. But neither of us is a professional photographer trained in making prints from turn-of-the-century glass plates. Consequently, we appreciate the contributions of photographer extraordinaire John Telford, our friend and colleague, whose work reminds us why George Edward Anderson's documentary photographs matter so much. John kindly consented to work with us when we approached him about participating in this undertaking. He finished printing the beautiful images contained in this book in June 2008.

William W. Slaughter, at the Church History Library in Salt Lake City, and Thomas R. Wells, of the L. Tom Perry Special Collections in the Harold B. Lee Library at Brigham Young University, facilitated the use of Anderson's original glass plates from their respective institutional collections so that John could print the photographs from the original glass plate negatives rather than using a copy of a copy. The fragile glass plates are a priceless treasure, some of the most valuable artifacts in the Church archives in Salt Lake City and at BYU. We know that John's reputation and professional credentials are the primary reason we were given access, and we are deeply appreciative. Use of the glass plates adds to the fresh approach that is the basis of this project and was the driving force behind our decision to spend time producing this volume.

Of course, John's work could not have been accomplished without research funds. We are grateful beyond measure to Victor and Carole Walch for their generous donation to BYU that allowed us to reprint the Anderson photographs from the original glass plates as Anderson had done in 1907. We recognize that there are many demands for the hard-earned financial resources in a family, especially in today's troubled economy. Everyone who now enjoys Anderson's photographs reprinted in this book is also blessed by the Walch family's munificent support for this project.

We acknowledge the efforts of many people, some unknown, who contributed to the preservation of the original Anderson glass plates. The plates could have easily vanished, just as so many artifacts from the past have been lost through neglect, fire and flood, and, in many cases, loved almost to death by much handling. Providentially, they were saved, catalogued, and preserved so that later generations could benefit from their existence. In recent years, others kept alive the memory of Anderson's important body of work, including T. Jeffery Cottle, Rell G. Francis (now deceased), Ted D. Stoddard, and Nelson B. Wadsworth. Each nurtured, encouraged, and collaborated in earlier efforts to learn more about Anderson and his work. Their kindness, support, and work continue to influence this particular project.

Additionally, we thank our friends and colleagues at the Religious Studies Center (RSC) at BYU who assisted us in completing this project, including R. Devan Jensen, who read the final draft of the manuscript and provided helpful comments that improved our writing and discussions; Brent Nordgren, who helped with the final photographs; and Joany Pinegar, who assisted with a host of items related to this book, including budgets, calendars, and student employees. RSC student employees, including Linda J. Bentley, Chris Keneipp, Alan Taylor Farnes, Berit Green, Erin Tanner Mecklenburg, and Rachael Moore, also assisted off and on for two and half years. One of the pleasures of our university assignment is to work with such bright, energetic student assistants.

Our writing efforts are based on the thoughtful work of many others who have attempted to tell the story of the Prophet Joseph Smith and the Church he organized under the direction of Jesus Christ. A list of particularly significant works that helped us shape these narratives is available in Sources at the end of this book. In addition, we are grateful beyond measure to those teachers, mentors, and colleagues who have shared their insights through their written works, personal conversations, and on-site visits to the places where the Restoration began to be unfolded more than one hundred and fifty years ago. And we are thankful beyond measure for Joseph Smith, his scribes, and others who put pen to paper to describe what they saw, heard, and felt during those events. Without their contributions, none of our work would have been possible.

We appreciate Deseret Book's continued interest in the story of the early Latter-day Saints and in Anderson's work. Cory Maxwell, Suzanne Brady, Shauna Gibby, and Tonya Facemyer have principally supported this particular project, for which we thank them.

Finally, we are grateful for George Edward Anderson's tireless efforts to document the history of the Church through his photographs. His was a labor of love, offered through years of toil and sacrifice. He gained neither wealth nor, during his lifetime, fame for his remarkable and singular contributions to capturing the past at Church history sites and to capturing Latter-day Saint life in Utah. We hope that this volume will focus more and well-deserved attention on the priceless record he created.

Prologue

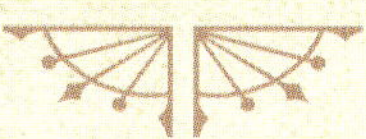

The large collection of photographic glass plates belonging to Utah-born photographer George Edward ("Ed") Anderson was made available to The Church of Jesus Christ of Latter-day Saints in the fall of 1928, a few months after his death. Junius F. Wells, assistant Church historian, described the nature and value of Anderson's images to Elder Joseph Fielding Smith, Church historian and member of the Quorum of the Twelve Apostles: "There are in this collection negatives of Church scenes . . . of inestimable interest and value to the Historian's Office." He observed that "George Ed. Anderson had performed a very remarkable mission while traversing the scenes of the Church History—the missions at the East and abroad, visiting hundreds of homes and neighborhoods where he bore a faithful testimony of the Truth and made countless friends for the Church."[1] The Church purchased the collection, and much of Anderson's lifelong work was saved for a future generation to appreciate and admire.

For many years, Anderson's photographs have been published, filling the pages of articles, essays, and book-long treatments of Church history without any acknowledgment of his creative efforts in providing dramatic views of Church history sites. Often we recognize the images, but we rarely know the name of the photographer or appreciate the personal sacrifices he and his family made to capture them. Anderson was absent from his Springville, Utah, home from 1907 until 1913, serving the Church and documenting its story, and his family finances seem to have always been a concern.

Anderson grew up just as photography was becoming another way to capture the past.

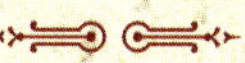

When Anderson left Utah for a mission in Great Britain in April 1907, he began a spiritual pilgrimage to the sites associated with the Restoration as he made his way east to begin his official mission in England. Born and raised in Utah, he knew the stories of the Restoration—the early history of The Church of Jesus Christ of Latter-day Saints. In many cases he had heard them from eyewitness participants, but the few visual images of the places where the remarkable events occurred came mostly through the artist's brush, sometimes from those who had not even been to the actual sites.

Anderson grew up just as photography was becoming another way to capture the past. He knew that his camera could miraculously freeze in time the scenes of the history of the Church. Soon, his proselytizing mission included another mission to systematically photograph historical sites in Missouri,

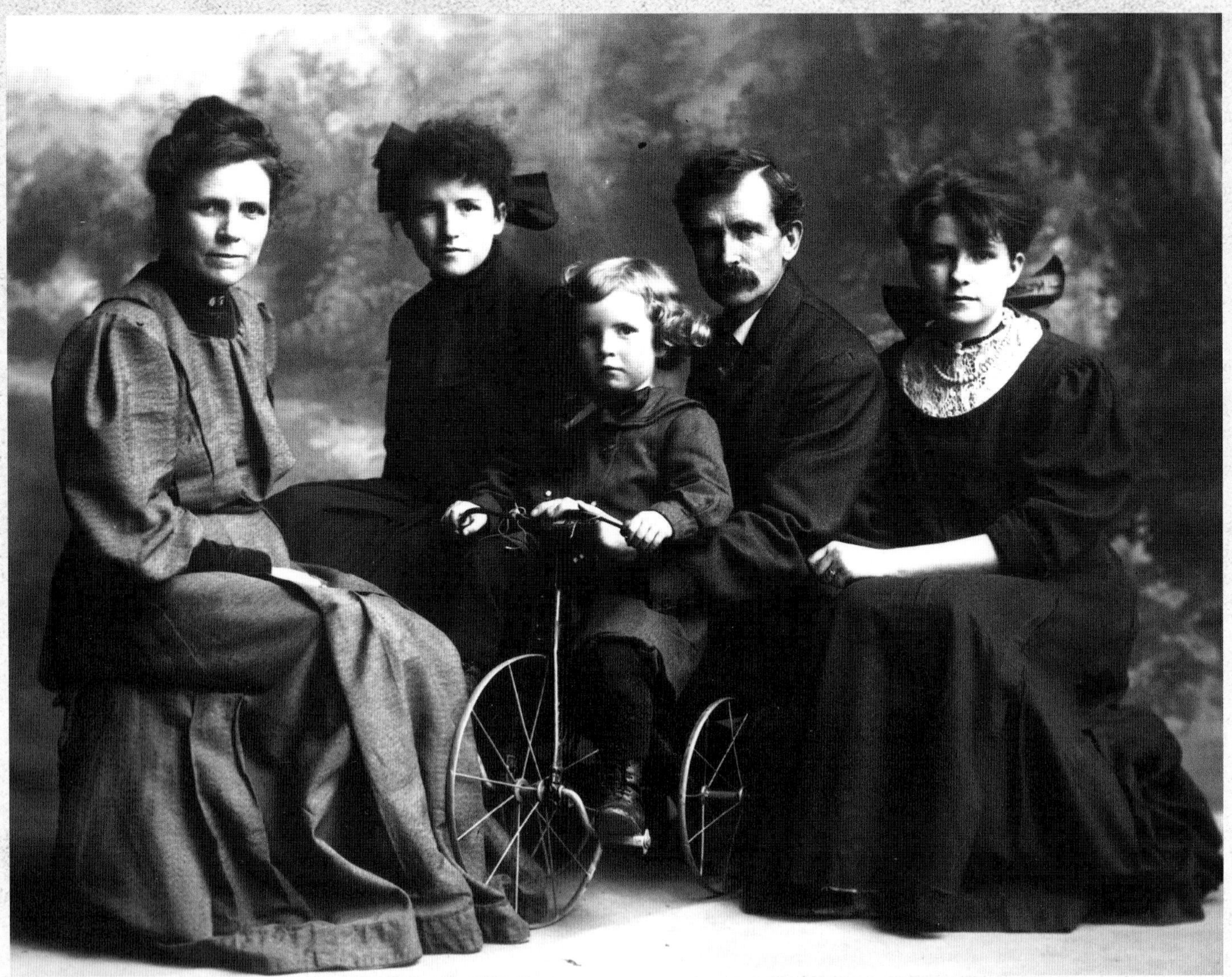

George Edward and Olive Lowry Anderson family, Springville, Utah, early 1907, Anderson Collection, L. Tom Perry Special Collections, Brigham Young University. Left to right: Olive Lowry, Edda, G. Lowry, George Edward, and Eva. This photograph was taken sometime before April 1907, when Anderson left on his mission to England.

Iowa, Illinois, Ohio, New York, Pennsylvania, and New England before he departed for England. Anderson understood the significance of his labors. He knew that the first Utah-born generation of Latter-day Saints, who generally could not travel to sites of transcendent events during the early years of the Restoration, would be blessed by visiting the sites through his photographs. The photographs would provide them a realistic and accurate view of these places of unimaginable significance.

Further, Anderson recognized that the nineteenth-century world of Joseph Smith and the early Saints was vanishing right before his eyes. The haunting images give a sense of what the preindustrial world—its rhythms, sights, sounds, and smells—was like for many early Saints. Nevertheless, Anderson's photographs capture the nation in transition. For example, we see telephone and electrical poles, streetcar tracks in roadways, and additions and changes to homes and buildings. Many of the images, however, preserve a world before concrete sidewalks and asphalt highways. In one sense, these photographs preserve aspects of the world as Joseph and Emma Smith saw it—a world much different from the one we witness today.

Yet Anderson knew that photography had its limits. He wrote in his diary, "Would like to get the views I can see in my mind's eye."[2] At one point he recorded, "Need the painter's hand to do it justice and fix the colors."[3] He also noted, "Could not get the effect of light and shade I wished."[4] Despite his recognition that photography at the time could not preserve the natural colors of the world he attempted to capture, his images are truly of "inestimable interest and value."

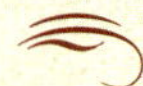

Photographer John Telford's work with the original glass plates allows us to see the photographs as Anderson originally printed them so many years ago. Relatively few have had that privilege. Although several of Anderson's photographs were printed in the *Boston Globe* on May 10, 1908, they were rendered in halftones of black and white. That is how his photographs continued to be published—until now. Recent advances in printing technology in combination with Telford's work with the original glass plates have made it possible to publish in this volume, for the very first time, reproductions of Anderson's images that are faithful to the tones he created.

Watching John practice the art of developing images from glass plates, almost exactly as Anderson did in 1907, was incredible. John worked in his lab with the glass plates, chemicals, and paper. He then took unexposed photographic paper outdoors to allow direct sunlight to expose the negative to the paper and miraculously bring the photograph to life. It was magical to watch an image appear on the paper through exposure to the sun. John then took the exposed prints back into the subdued light of his darkroom and immersed them in a series of trays containing various chemicals and water for final processing.

Anderson's images have been reproduced endlessly in black and white, but seeing them as he originally produced them, in the warm tones captured in this book, we recognize the aesthetic value of these amazing images. They help us to realize that the early history of the Church took place in specific geographical locations—places where the Saints laughed, cried, lived, and died. We hope our small effort, along with that of many others, may help to permanently establish Anderson's remarkable and singular contribution to preserving the story of the Restoration through his amazing photographic record.

Anderson recognized that the nineteenth-century world of Joseph Smith and the early Saints was vanishing right before his eyes. Many of the images preserve a world before concrete sidewalks and asphalt highways.

In the end, Anderson's photographs bear witness to the events that drew him to these sacred places in the first place. They remind us of the early days of the Restoration, "days never to be forgotten" (Joseph Smith–History 1:71n), when men and women again began to hear the voices of angels, the Savior, and our Heavenly Father; days that saw the start of the dispensation of the fulness of times, during which "old men shall dream dreams, your young men shall see visions: and also upon the servants and upon the handmaids in those days will I pour out my spirit" (Joel 2:28–29); days when the Lord again began to invite God's children throughout the world, "Come unto me, all ye that labour and are heavy laden, and I will give you rest" (Matthew 11:28).

Introduction

Glass Plates and Pen, Paper, and Ink

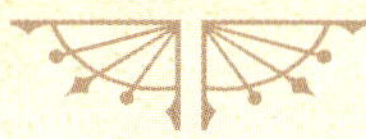

The Lord spoke to Joseph Smith the very day the Church of Jesus Christ was organized on April 6, 1830, saying, "Behold, there shall be a record kept among you" (D&C 21:1). Because of this commandment, the Prophet (and his scribes and clerks) spent time during his incredibly busy ministry to prepare thousands of pages of materials that make up the record of his life, ministry, and the early history of the Church. This remarkable collection includes personal diaries, historical narratives, revelations, translations, letters, and other official documents.[1]

Despite producing a significant collection of important historical material during his lifetime, Joseph Smith often felt frustrated in his efforts to fulfill the commandment to keep a record. In November 1832 the Prophet reflected, "O Lord God deliver us in thy due time from the little narrow prison almost as it were total darkness of paper pen and ink and a crooked broken scattered and imperfect language."[2] Several additional factors impinged on his early efforts to produce a comprehensive record, including limited financial resources, various moves (New York, Ohio, Missouri, and Illinois) that often resulted from violent extralegal actions by mobs, and the daily burdens and duties associated with leading the Church.

> The Prophet (and his scribes and clerks) spent time during his incredibly busy ministry to prepare thousands of pages of materials that make up the record of his life, ministry, and the early history of the Church.

Given the realities of the Prophet's life in the first half of the nineteenth century, it is remarkable that we have as many records as we do. Nevertheless, historians and Church members wish they had more. For example, Joseph Smith spoke in public and private on numerous occasions. It is generally agreed, however, that we have only about 10 percent of his discourses, and these records are mostly brief notations, preserving no more than a fraction of what he said on the occasion.[3]

Additionally, some key historical dates of the Restoration have been lost because a record was not made at the time (for example, the dates of the First Vision and the restoration of the Melchizedek Priesthood were not preserved). In some cases we have only brief references to what would be for anyone a singular event. We do not know, for example, when "Michael [appeared] on the banks of the Susquehanna" or when Joseph heard "the voice of Gabriel, and of Raphael, and of divers angels" (D&C 128:20–21). These and other transcendent events are significant even though we do not know more details, including dates or precise locations.

In February 1835 the Prophet acknowledged the consequence of failing to record important events and meetings. "It is a fact (said President Smith) that if I now had in my possession, every decision which has been had upon important items of doctrine and duties which have been given since the commencement of this work, I would not part with it for any sum of money; but we have neglected to take minutes of such things, thinking, perhaps, that they would never benefit us afterwards; which, if we had them now, would decide almost every point of doctrine."[4]

The Church's efforts to fulfill the Lord's command to keep a record did not end with the Prophet's death on June 27, 1844. Dedicated Church leaders who had been associates and close friends of the Prophet—including Willard Richards (1804–54), George A. Smith (1817–75), and Wilford Woodruff (1807–98)—and a number of lay historians, some of whom had not known Joseph Smith personally, labored diligently and tirelessly to preserve Joseph Smith's history and the story of the Church through the nineteenth century. They did so despite the challenges of the exodus from Nauvoo and the physically demanding efforts to gather and settle the Saints and build a religious community in the Mountain West.[5] During the twentieth century, their important work became the foundation of continued efforts by an increasing number of individuals and institutions to tell the story of the Latter-day Saints.

Eventually, the Church employed professionally trained archivists, historians, and museum curators to help fulfill the Lord's command. Working under the direction of Church leaders, including the Church historian, these men and women collected, documented, and interpreted the story of the Restoration. Their contributions, usually unknown to most people, have blessed our lives in remarkable ways. Added to their efforts were those of a number of Latter-day Saint and other scholars interested not only in the story of the restored Church of Jesus Christ but also in the context of the Restoration in the larger field of American religious history. All in all, Mormon history has a remarkable life itself.

> The Church now employs professionally trained archivists, historians, and curators to help fulfill the Lord's command.

A number of important books and articles continue to offer fresh perspectives on the story of Joseph Smith and the early Church. The work of dedicated and thoughtful scholars is bringing into focus important topics, individuals, and events that deepen our understanding of and appreciation for the story of the Latter-day Saints. New archaeological investigations at Church historical sites—including the Smith family log home in Palmyra and Joseph Smith's Red Brick Store in Nauvoo—and the discovery of previously unknown primary sources—the 1828–34 manuscript "Book of Commandments and Revelations," for example—allow us to reexamine old data so we can better appreciate and understand the past in its context. It truly is an exciting time to be alive when so much work from a variety of perspectives and disciplines is shedding additional light on our sacred history.

Another important contribution to preserving our sacred past was performed by photographers. They provide another type of primary sources: visual images of sites before modern developments transformed them and of people who were part of the story at those sacred places. Lucian R. Foster (1806–?), Marsena Cannon (1812–1900), William A. Smith (1825–97), Charles R. Savage (1832–1909), Charles W. Carter (1832–1918), and George Edward Anderson (1860–1928) produced the earliest images of individual Mormons and sites associated with their story.[6]

> When Anderson finally returned to Utah, he had collected an amazing documentary record.

Anderson was the first Latter-day Saint professional photographer to document early Church historical sites in New England, New York, Pennsylvania, Ohio, Missouri, and Illinois. Leaving from Springville, Utah, for a mission to the British Isles in April 1907, he took his heavy eight-by-ten view camera, supplies (including a set of glass plates), and personal belongings. His camera, also known as a large-format camera, accommodated eight-by-ten-inch glass plates (hence "large-format") and was always used with a tripod. Together, the camera and the tripod weighed between fifteen and twenty pounds, far different from the five- to eight-ounce, point-and-shoot digital cameras used today.

As he made his way east, Anderson visited and photographed sites of the important and transcendent events in the story of The Church of Jesus Christ of Latter-day Saints. He desired to provide a visual record for a Utah-born generation that had heard the stories of the early Saints but generally was unable to visit the actual sites. When he finally returned to Utah in November 1913, nearly seven years later, he had collected an amazing documentary record of the Sacred Grove in New York, the Kirtland Temple in Ohio, Joseph Smith's Nauvoo home in Illinois, and the Independence Temple site in Missouri.

Historic photographs have only recently taken their appropriate place as an important source for reconstructing the past. At first, photographs were added to thoughtful, well-crafted essays or books almost as an afterthought. Sometimes the author was not involved in selecting and placing the images or in preparing the captions. Today, more than ever, authors consider historic photographs an important part of their efforts to tell their story. More attention is being given to providing proper documentation of photographs when published. Some scholars have learned how to *read* a photograph just as they read any other type of documentary source. They use historic photographs as a vital way to tell their story.

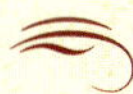

This volume thus has two separate but related purposes. The first is to provide readers for the first time the experience of seeing Anderson's important photographs of Church historical sites as he himself printed them rather than in the ubiquitous black-and-white form we have become accustomed to seeing during the past seventy-five years.

The second is to provide a fresh, crisp take on Church history sites that drew Anderson to photograph them in the first place. Narrative chapters introduce Joseph Smith's own history and the early history of the Church in New England, New York, Pennsylvania, Ohio, Missouri, and Illinois. These chapters incorporate some of the latest findings, insights, and interpretations of the events and people who made history in places now sacred to the Latter-day Saints. Covering a familiar storyline, these narratives provide readers the same kind of experience they will certainly have when they see Anderson's photographs as he printed them originally. Many details are familiar, but subtle nuances bring the story into new focus and allow us to explore new angles previously overlooked.

1

George Edward Anderson's Photography

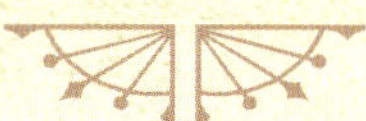

by John Telford

George Edward Anderson's photographs of Latter-day Saint historical sites were all made on gelatin dry-plate glass negatives that were either eight-by-ten inches or five-by-seven inches. His diary makes frequent reference to his "instrument," or his camera, but gives no information as to make, size, or other details. It is obvious, however, that the camera was at least eight-by-ten inches and probably had multiple backs to accommodate both eight-by-ten-inch and five-by-seven-inch glass plates. Anderson would have used a large black focusing cloth so that he could see the image on the ground-glass viewfinder of the large camera. The camera, of course, was placed on a sturdy tripod. Critical adjustments for composition and focus were made while he was under the focusing cloth.

Anderson relied solely on experience in calculating exposure because no exposure meters had been created by 1907.

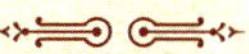

The light-sensitive plates would be placed in light-tight plate holders (referred to as film holders today) that would be inserted into the back of the camera after all the adjustments had been made and the exposure had been calculated. Anderson relied solely on experience in calculating exposure because no exposure meters had been created by 1907. But it is obvious that his calculations were not always accurate because he makes frequent reference to "reducing" and "intensifying" (corrective measures to adjust the density of the negatives before making prints) after the negatives had been developed. Once in place in the back of the camera, a black slide would be pulled out of the plate holder, exposing the light-sensitive glass plate to the image-forming light emitted by the camera lens. Each time Anderson refers to "making a view," he followed this cumbersome and time-consuming procedure.

An interesting question to consider is why, in 1907, did Anderson choose to use an eight-by-ten camera and glass plate negatives at all? Why did he choose to go through the cumbersome procedure of setting up the large-format camera and tripod, disappearing under a black focusing cloth to make tedious adjustments and finally an exposure, and then locating a darkroom where he could individually develop each glass plate negative? He was aware of the technical advances that had been made by George Eastman. By 1890 flexible film and the handheld camera had been introduced. Daylight-loading roll film and folding hand cameras were available by 1896. That meant that not only were reasonably good cameras available but also that photographers could

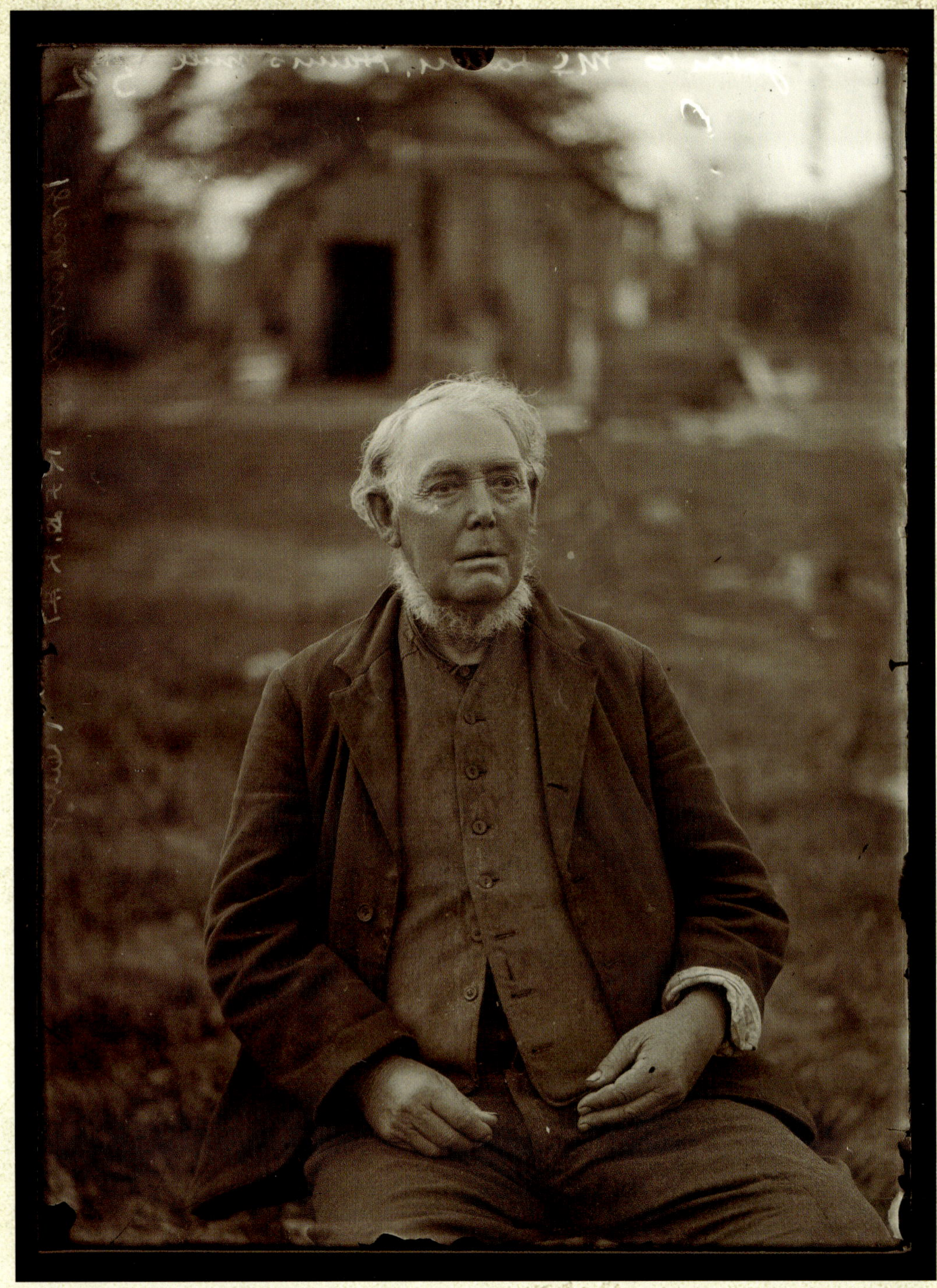

John B. McLallen, who hosted Latter-day Saint missionaries and George Edward Anderson, Breckenridge, Missouri, May 22, 1907, Anderson Collection, L. Tom Perry Special Collections, Brigham Young University, Provo, Utah.

develop their own roll film. The influential photographer Alfred Stieglitz had been using a handheld camera since 1896, and splendid reproductions of important photographic accomplishments were published in both his *Camera Notes* and *Camera Works* magazines by the early 1900s.

These advances popularized the camera, as illustrated in an 1894 diary entry by Utah photographer C. R. Savage, Anderson's mentor: "Not doing much viewing [photographing] lately. . . . Nearly everybody is becoming a photographer. Business is changing to developing and finishing views for amateurs. Most of the magazines now published are illustrated by photo engravings—the demand for views is gradually falling off."[1]

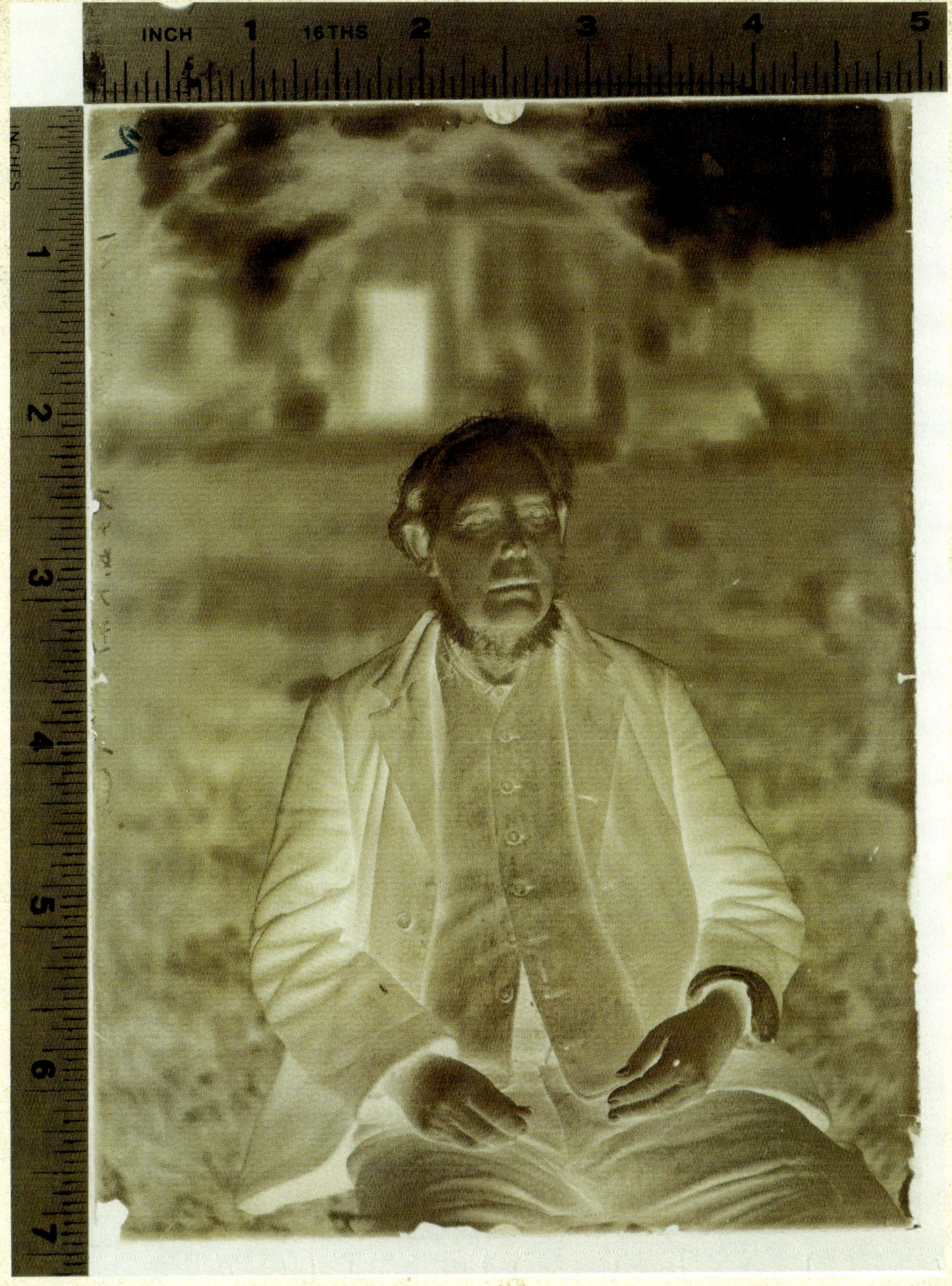

John B. McLallen, five-by-seven-inch glass plate negative, Anderson Collection, L. Tom Perry Special Collections, Brigham Young University, Provo, Utah.

In the June 8, 1907, entry in his diary, Anderson wrote, "In the evening, gave Elder Curtis a lesson on his Kodak," indicating that Anderson was familiar with the increasingly popular handheld camera that Eastman Kodak Company was producing at the time.[2]

Another equally interesting question to consider is Anderson's aesthetic standard. Two major aesthetic camps, the "art photographers" and the "scientific photographers," dominated photography at the turn of the century. The art photographers were following a major worldwide movement known as pictorialism, which coincided with the impressionist movement in painting. Pictorialism was a photographic movement or school of thought used to describe images that emphasized the artistic quality of the photograph rather than the scene it depicted. It was defined by soft-focus images of nostalgic landscapes, wistful portraits, and elusive print-making processes such as platinum, gum-bichromate, carbon, and bromoil.

Art photographers were critical of scientific photographers, whom they labeled as fact finders who made sharp, highly detailed photographs on glossy gelatin silver paper. Stieglitz, who had been a major influence in the pictorialist movement, started the Photo-Secessionists of New York in 1902 to promote photography as a fine art.

Anderson used eight-by-ten-inch glass plate negatives in 1907 for quality and precision.

One standard, or quality, easily deciphers Anderson's aesthetics as well as his technical decisions. While it is possible that he chose to use an eight-by-ten camera and glass plate negatives based on his familiarity with them, it is unlikely that was the main reason for his decision. He was, after all, experimenting with new "develop-out paper" for making prints rather than the printing-out paper that was more commonly used at the time. His technical choice of the eight-by-ten camera also defines his aesthetic choice—precision, detail, and quality. Just as photographers today choose to use large-format cameras because of their quality and precision rather than smaller, more easily operating cameras, Anderson chose to use eight-by-ten glass plate negatives in 1907 because of quality and precision. He chose to make sharp, highly detailed images of important Latter-day Saint historical sites based on a desire to show information and facts about those important sites.

Anderson chose an eight-by-ten camera, glass plate negatives, and glossy prints to show fine detail, but he retouched photos to soften detail. Anderson makes frequent reference to "spotting" the negatives. Contemporary use of the term *spotting* refers to filling in spots and scratches frequently found on the print but occasionally seen in the negative. An examination of one of Anderson's negatives, however, often reveals substantial work done to soften the lines and wrinkles on the subject's face.

The photograph of John B. McLallen taken at Haun's Mill is a good example. The glass plate is five-by-seven inches. When lit from behind, the negative shows no evidence of retouching; however, when it is illuminated with oblique light, on the emulsion side of the negative an oval of retouching compound can be seen around the subject's face. Within that oval are several pencil marks used to soften the wrinkles and lines on Mr. McLallen's aging face. Lines under the eyes, around the nose and cheeks, and on the chin have been softened. A few dust spots, seen as white spots on the negative, have not been touched or spotted.

Also seen on the edges of the negative is Anderson's inscription: "John B McLallen, Haun's Mill Breckenridge RFDR #1." On the image area itself, lightly written in pencil at a later date by a librarian, is "14363 John B. McLallen Hauns Mill." "Hauns" is clearly seen in the example shown on page 10. On the finished print, however, only the inscription written by Anderson is seen on the edges. It is backward because it is written on the emulsion side of the glass plate, which, when printed, is on the backward side of the negative (see examples of McLallen negatives on pages 11 and 13).

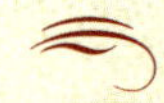

All of this demonstrates that George Edward Anderson was first and foremost a successful portrait photographer. As such he was continually appealing to the vanity of his subjects

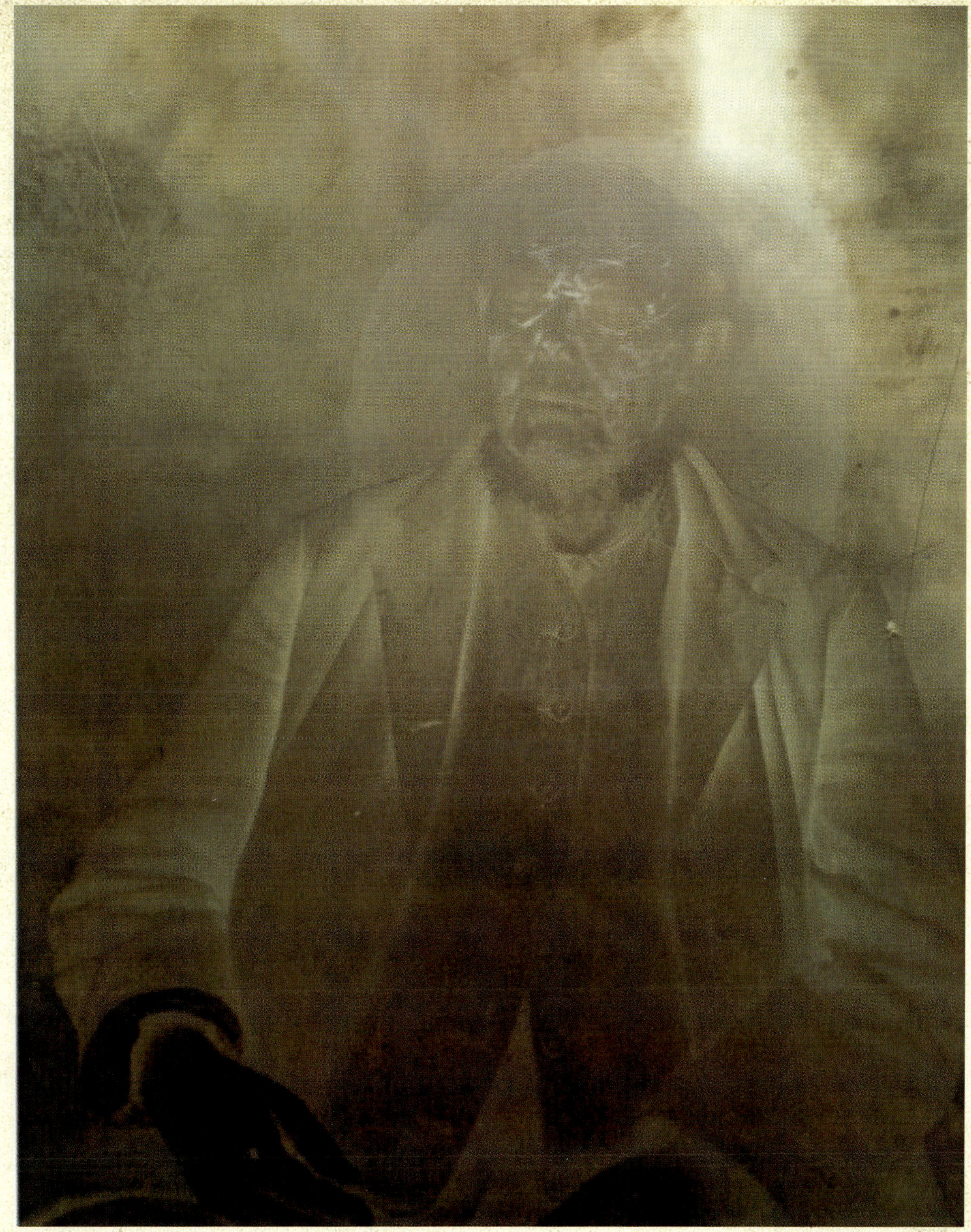

John B. McLallen, negative illuminated with oblique light that reveals an oval of retouching compound around the subject's head and several pencil marks used to soften wrinkles and lines on his face, Anderson Collection, L. Tom Perry Special Collections, Brigham Young University, Provo, Utah.

by retouching perceived imperfections in their faces. And while he used the large-format camera to show detail and precision, he softened that detail and precision when it became unflattering to his subjects. This may also add to an understanding of his use of eight-by-ten and five-by-seven glass plates. They were simply much easier to retouch.

In his diary, Anderson refers to making prints using Azo develop-out paper. The develop-out process, new to Anderson in 1907, is the most common procedure for making traditional nondigital black and white prints today. The photographic paper is exposed to light, which forms an invisible latent image. The image is made visible by immersing the paper in a developer and then placing it in a chemical bath that renders the print insensitive to light. Toning the print alters the resulting color and increases the longevity, or archival stability, of the photograph.

The problems of yellowing that Anderson describes in his diary are typically a result of poor or insufficient fixing. The yellowing may also have occurred when the prints were subsequently toned. The develop-out process was difficult to master because of the increased light sensitivity of the paper and the demands of precise processing at each step. Azo paper, recently discontinued by Kodak, was specifically designed for contact printing, meaning that the print is exposed while in direct contact with the negative, resulting in a print that is the same size as the negative. The "gaslight" spoken of by Anderson was an artificial light source, typically a gas flame. Prints, therefore, could be made at night using the artificial light source.

The process Anderson had been using before 1907, and with which he was much more familiar, was the printing-out process. Prints were still made by contact but were made by prolonged exposure to daylight, typically direct sunlight. The image was formed by the direct agency of light with no development required. The resulting print had a reddish-brown color made up of filamentary silver particles. The gelatin silver chloride printing-out paper, also known as POP or Solio paper, was for many decades one of the standard printing papers of the industry. POP paper was introduced in Germany in 1884, and by the mid-1890s no fewer than eight American and at least as many European companies manufactured it. The process was familiar to Anderson, but it is nearly unknown to photographers today.

The prints for *Through the Lens* were made using the POP process. Each print was made by placing the photographic paper in contact with the original glass plate negative in a contact-printing frame and exposing it to direct sunlight for an average of five minutes. Some of the negatives required as little as one minute of exposure; others required as much as twenty minutes. The contact-printing frame was designed with a split-hinged back so that during exposure the print could be taken to a shaded area and inspected by opening the hinged portion of the frame, pulling the print away from a portion of the negative, and checking the density, or exposure, of the print. The exposure started as a weak purple color and progressed minute by minute to a darker, more reddish color.

The prints for *Through the Lens* were made by placing photographic paper in contact with the original glass plate negatives in a frame and exposing them to direct sunlight for an average of five minutes.

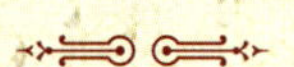

The fully exposed print, much darker than the desired final print, was removed from the printing frame and immersed in warm water. A milky substance, excess silver chloride, was released from the print. After three or four changes of water, the milky release ceased. The print was then immersed in a toning bath of gold-chloride and ammonium thiocyanate. Filamentary silver particles are relatively smaller, and therefore less stable and less permanent, than physically developed silver particles. To correct this deficiency, the silver was toned with gold, which rendered the silver inert, or permanent. The gold-chloride also changed the color of the print. Depending on the amount of toning, the resulting print color may range from brown to purple.

After the toning bath, each print was fixed in a mild, nonacid fixing bath made of sodium thiosulfate (called *fixer* or *hypo*) crystals that removed any remaining light-sensitive silver chloride particles. (Those familiar with contemporary develop-out processing will note that while the toning of a print is done after fixing and washing in contemporary procedures, they are reversed in the printing-out process.) The final print was then washed for thirty to sixty minutes and air dried on screens designed for that purpose.

Each of the processing steps—washing, toning, fixing, and final washing—lightened the print. Therefore, it was overprinted, or printed darker than desired, to compensate for the subsequent lightening during processing. The final color, tonality, and exposure were not realized until the print was completely dry; therefore, good judgment in exposure and toning was critical in the printing procedure.

The final prints are rich with detail, tonality, and beautiful red to brown (sepia) colors. They are a fitting tribute to George Edward Anderson's monumental photographic work.

2

New England

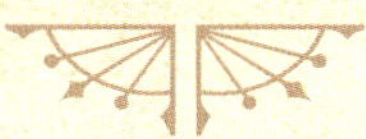

George Edward Anderson's photographs of various sites in Vermont are an unmistakable acknowledgment of the role the state played in the family history and early life of Joseph Smith. Best known to many Latter-day Saints, perhaps, as the birthplace of the Prophet, Vermont was also the state where his parents, Joseph Smith Sr. and Lucy Mack, met and married and where eight of his siblings were born. Vermont witnessed some of the more difficult times for the Smith family, including the crop failures and financial reverses that precipitated the move to upstate New York. Having lived in Vermont for nine years as a child, Joseph considered himself a "Green Mountain Boy" at heart long after his prophetic calling took him elsewhere.[1]

The two trips Anderson took to Tunbridge, Vermont, for pictures—once in the dead of winter—underscore that it was here that the story of the Smith family begins. In the fall of 1791, at age twenty, Joseph Sr. moved to Tunbridge from Ipswich, Massachusetts, with his father, Asael, his mother, Mary, and his ten siblings. The family settled on an eighty-three-acre farm in the "gore," three miles northwest of the village of South Tunbridge.[2] While here, the family met and befriended Stephen Mack—older brother of Lucy Mack—who ran a "mercantile and tinning business" in the area.[3] Lucy met Joseph Sr. during an extended visit to her brother following the death of her sister Lovina, and the two were married on January 24, 1796, in Tunbridge. Following their marriage, the couple took over the farm in the gore while Asael and the rest of the family moved to another farm nearby. Here Joseph and Lucy lived until 1802, during which time they brought three children into the world: an unnamed son who died at birth, Alvin (born February 11, 1798), and Hyrum (born February 9, 1800). It was also in Tunbridge, a year after his marriage, that Joseph helped his father and brother Jesse found a Universalist society.[4]

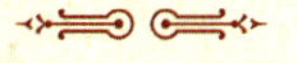

The two trips Anderson took to Tunbridge, Vermont, for pictures underscore that it was here that the story of the Smith family begins.

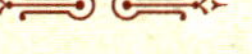

In 1802, Joseph and Lucy rented out the farm and moved to Randolph to try their hand at running a store. By the end of the year, they were back on the farm in Tunbridge, where Sophronia was born the following year (May 16, 1803) and where Lucy first became "deeply impressed with the subject of religion."[5] Having been defrauded in a business venture, Joseph Sr. was forced to sell

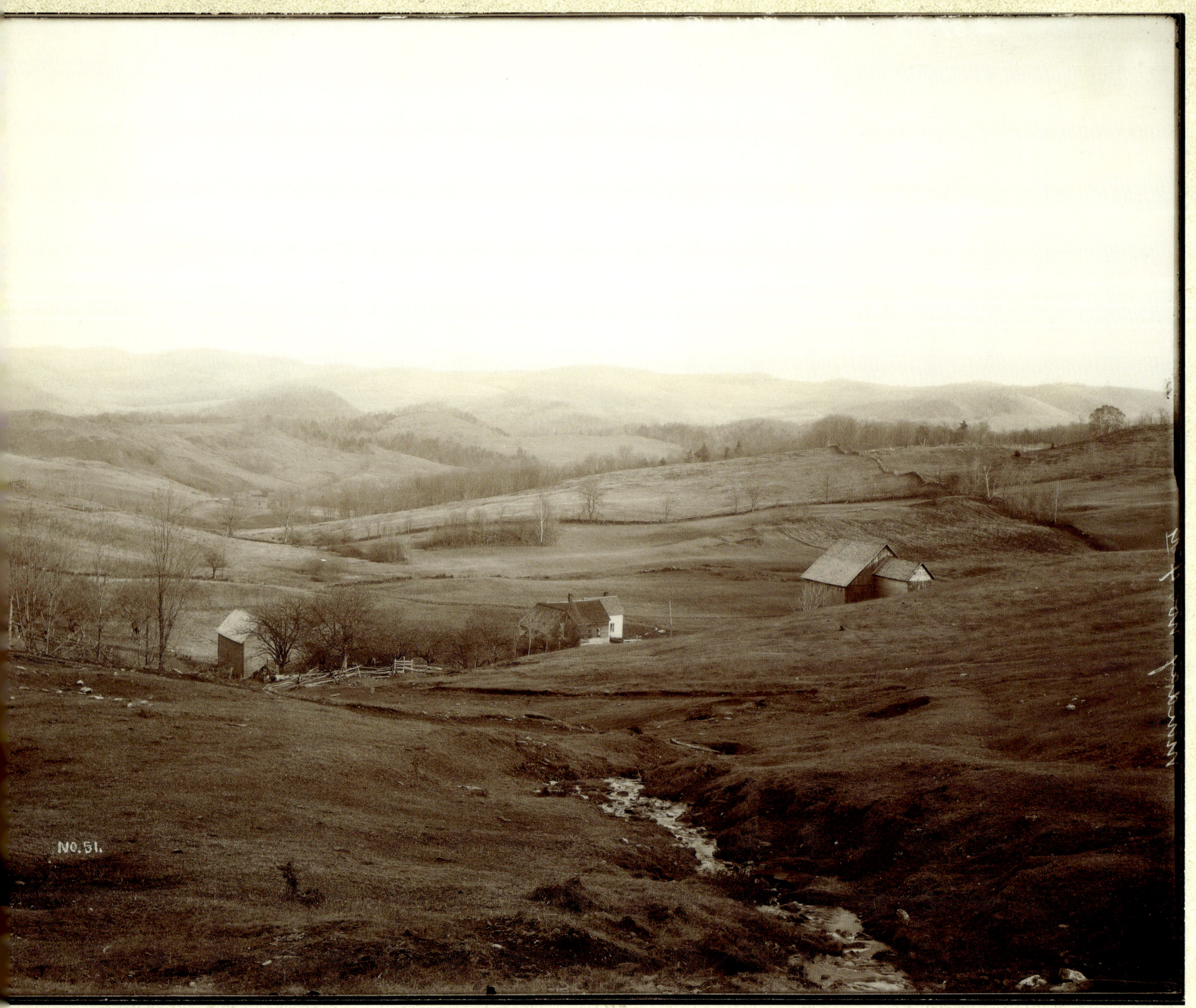

Tunbridge Gore, Vermont, 1907, Anderson Collection, LDS Church History Library, Salt Lake City, Utah.

the Tunbridge farm a short time later. The family soon moved to Royalton and then to Sharon, Vermont, where Lucy gave birth to her fifth child, Joseph, on December 23, 1805. During a final brief stay in Tunbridge after their three-year sojourn in Sharon, she gave birth to Samuel Harrison on March 13, 1808.

Unable to purchase a place of their own after the loss of the Tunbridge farm, the Smiths lived in a log cabin they rented in Sharon from Lucy's father, Solomon Mack, and farmed sixty-eight of the one hundred acres Solomon had purchased in August 1804[6]—circumstances somewhat obscured by the

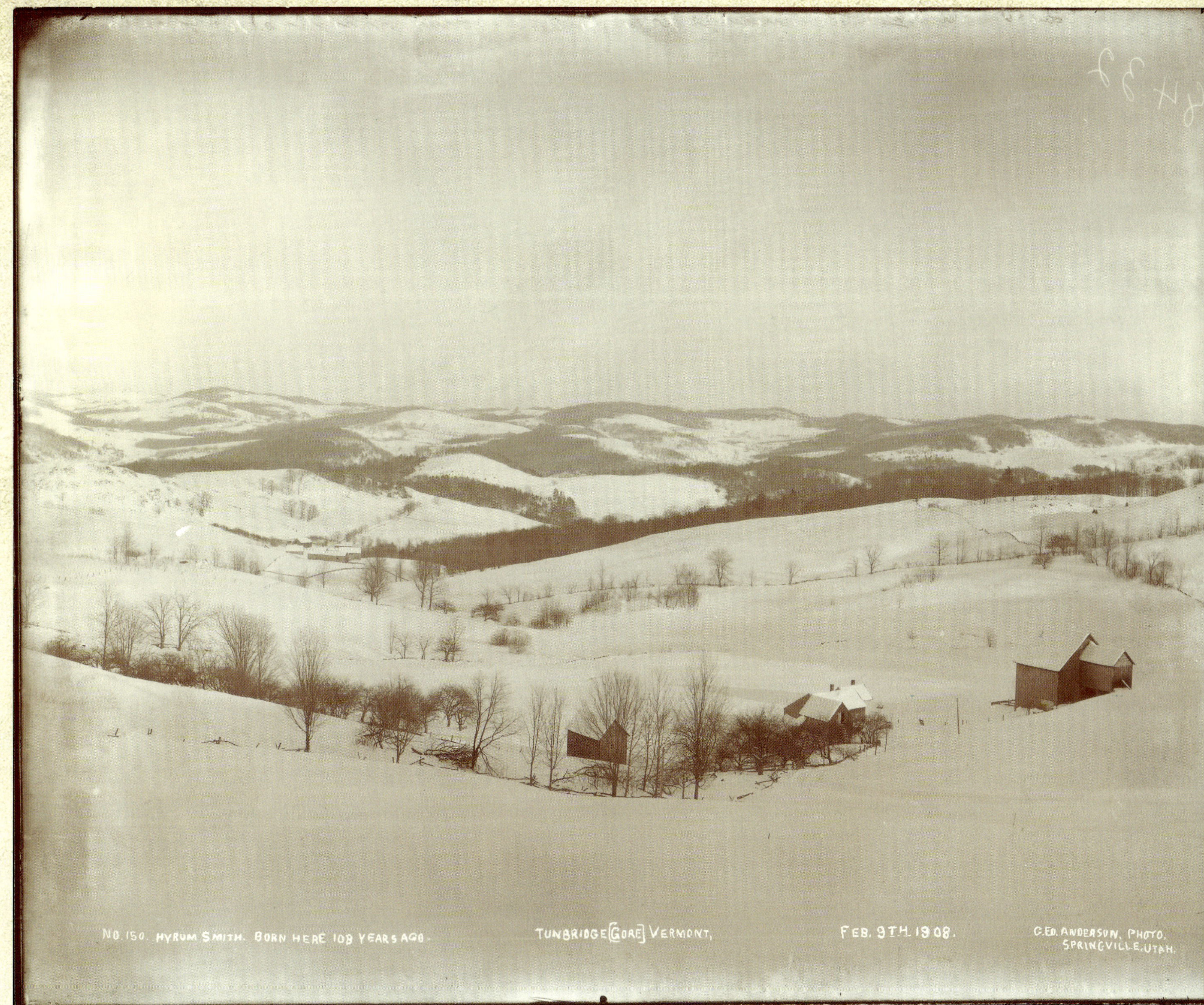

Tunbridge Gore, Vermont, February 9, 1908, Anderson Collection, LDS Church History Library, Salt Lake City, Utah.

beautiful Memorial Cottage and the Joseph Smith Memorial Monument that Anderson photographed more than a hundred years later. To make ends meet, Joseph Sr. also taught school the three winters they were in Sharon. The family's diligence and frugality paid off, with Lucy reporting later that over the course of the family's time in Sharon, "our circumstances gradually improved, until we found ourselves quite comfortable again."[7]

Following moves to Royalton, Vermont, and Lebanon, New Hampshire, the Smiths moved to Norwich, Vermont, apparently in time for spring planting in 1814. Eight-year-old

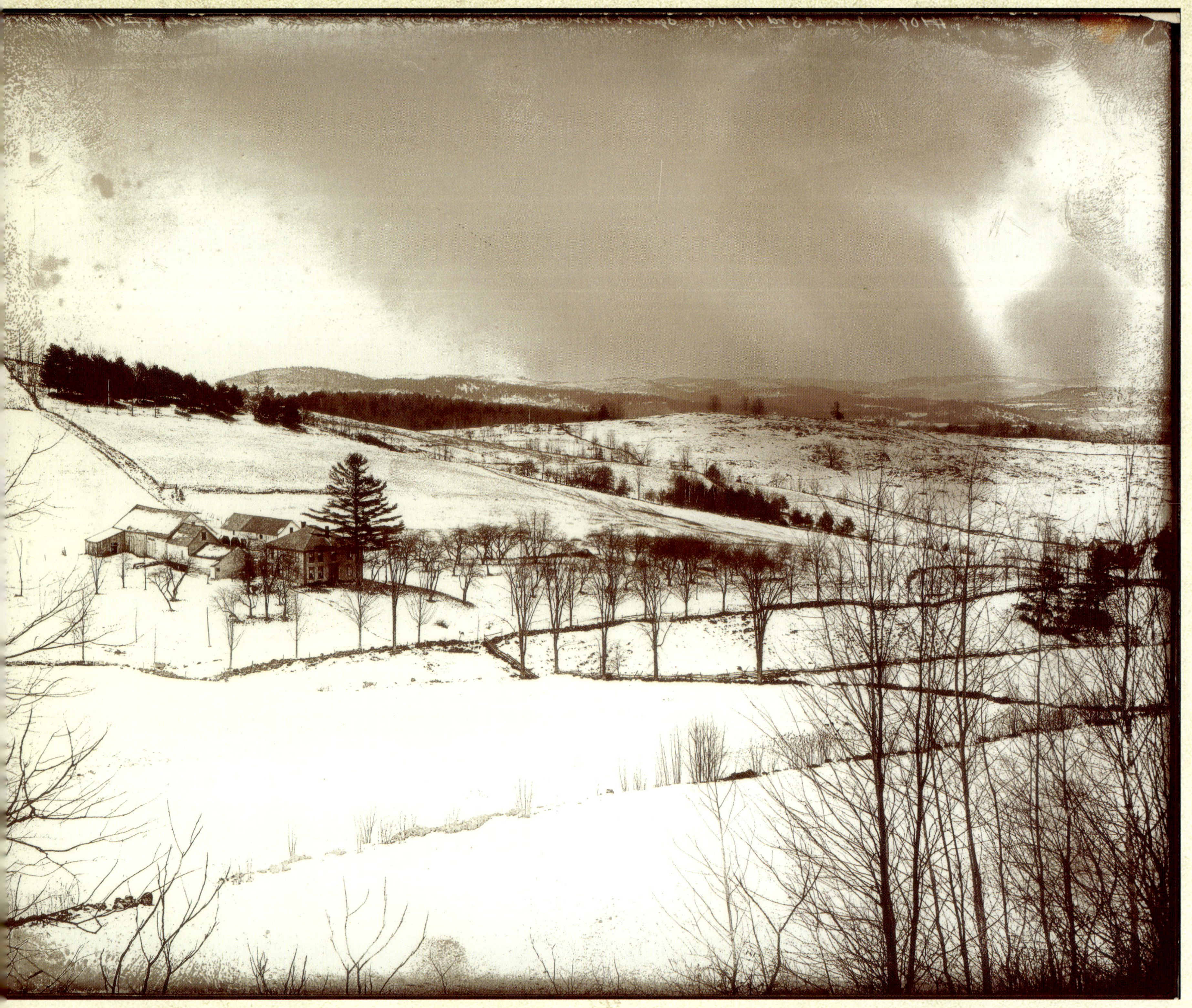

Squire Murdock's farm, Norwich, Vermont, January 23, 1908, Anderson Collection, LDS Church History Library, Salt Lake City, Utah.

Joseph was on crutches at the time, recuperating from surgery the previous year for osteomyelitis in his leg.

In Norwich, the Smiths rented 140 acres from Squire Constant Murdock, who owned several farms in the area. Here the Smiths' fortunes took another turn for the worse when their first year's crops failed. After sustaining themselves for a year with "considerable exertion," the Smiths managed to plant a crop the next year.[8] This crop also failed, probably as a result of a global cooling trend that had been underway for several years.

Concerned that the Smiths might prove a burden on the

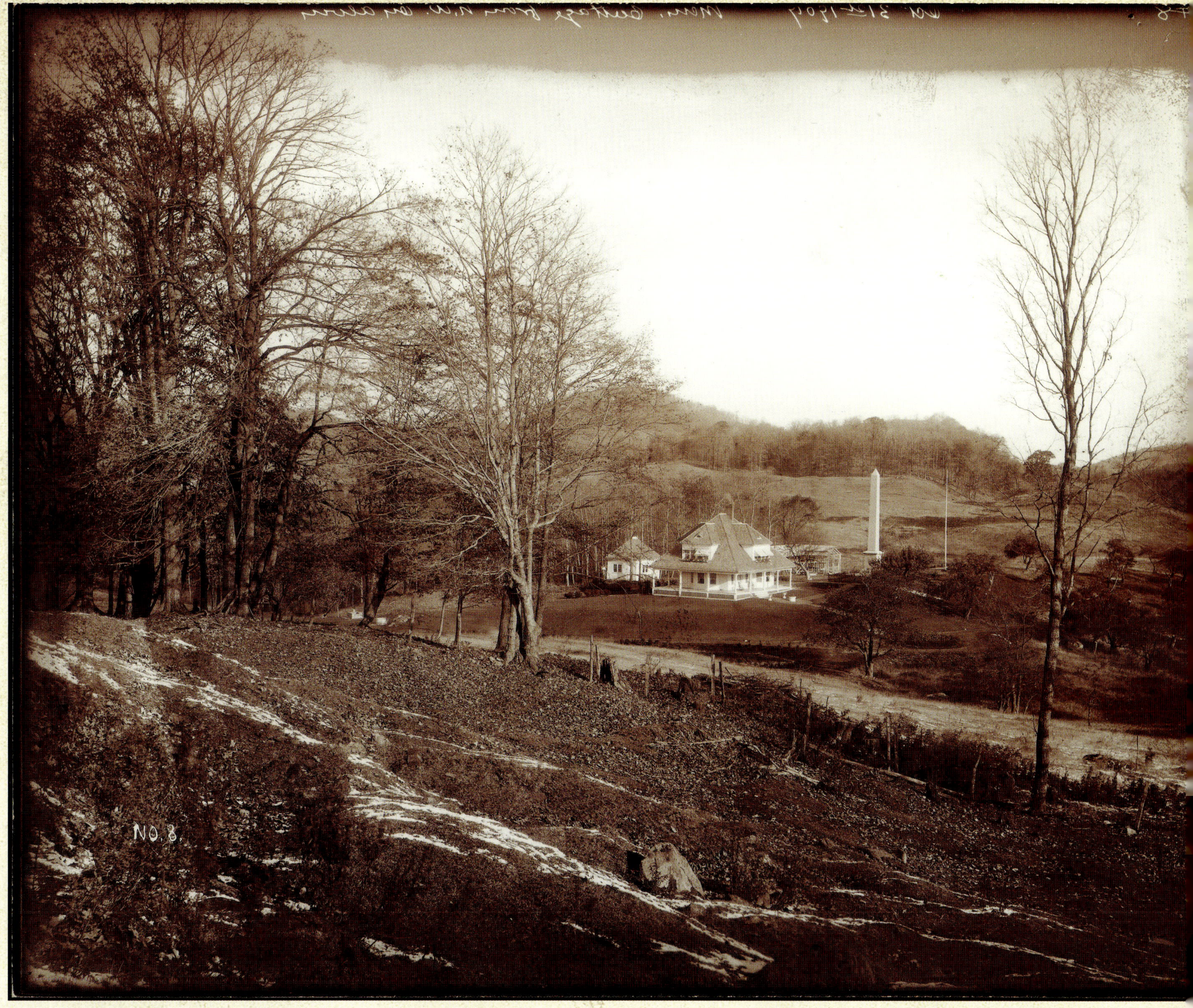

Memorial Cottage and the Joseph Smith Memorial Monument, Sharon, Vermont, October 31, 1907, Anderson Collection, LDS Church History Library, Salt Lake City, Utah.

resources of the town, Norwich authorities formally "warned out" the family on May 15, 1816—a not-so-polite way of inviting indigent-looking newcomers to take their financial problems elsewhere.[9] Staking everything on a successful harvest in 1816, Joseph Sr. planted one more time, determined that "if he should meet with no better success than he had the two preceding years, he would then go to the state of New York, where wheat was raised in abundance."[10]

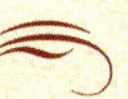

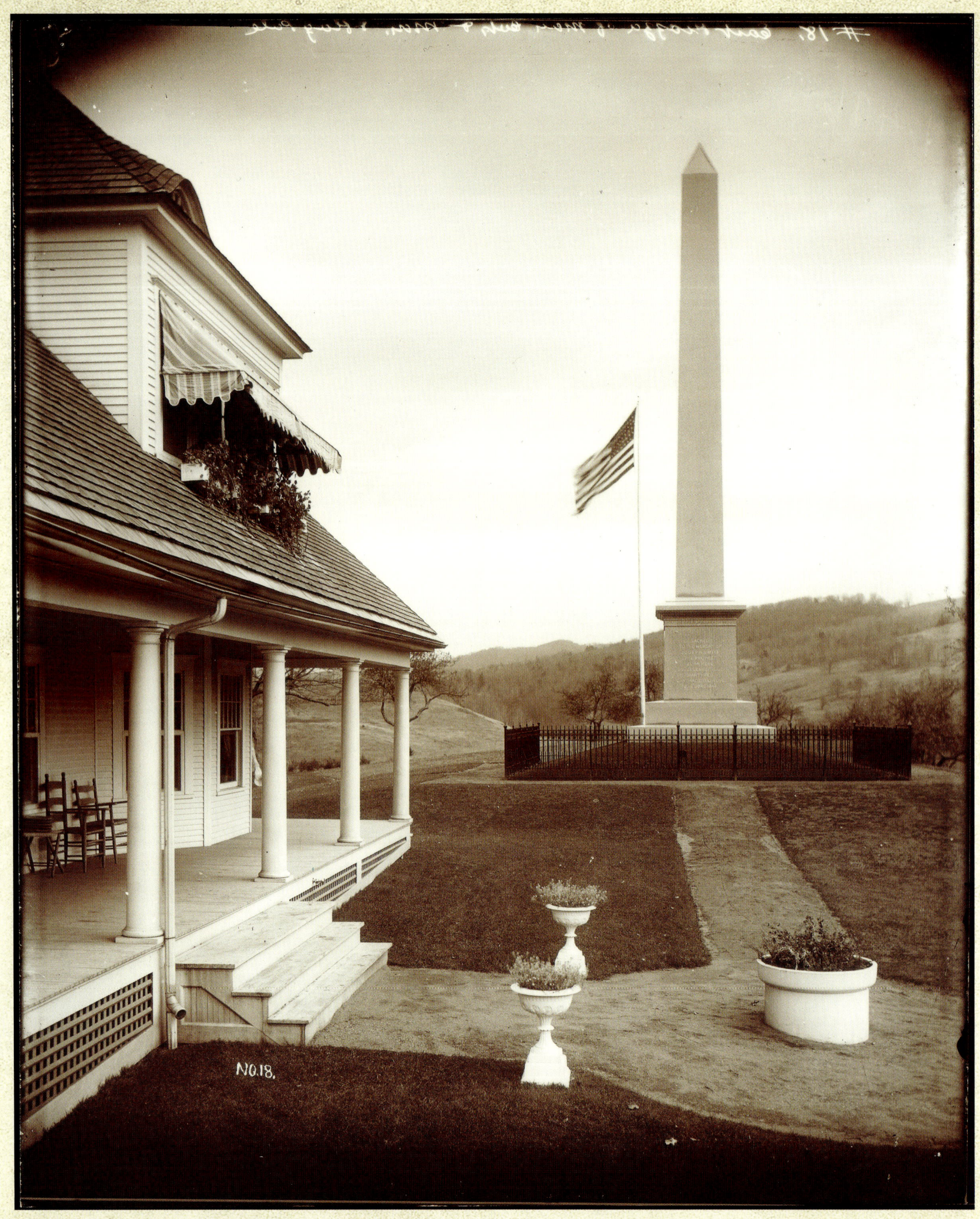

Joseph Smith Memorial Monument, Sharon, Vermont, 1907, Anderson Collection, LDS Church History Library, Salt Lake City, Utah.

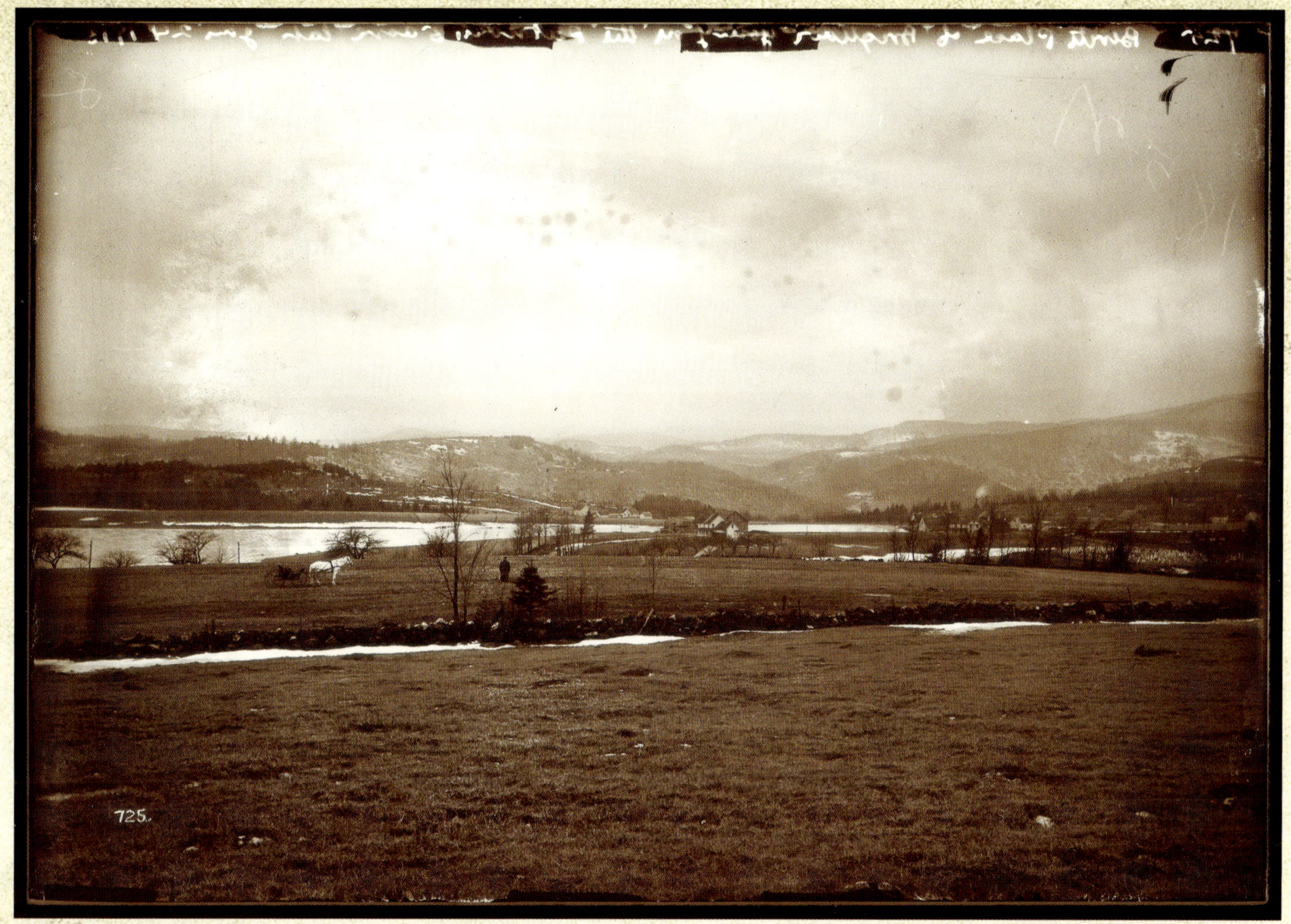

Putnam's five-acre lot, the traditional site of Brigham Young's birthplace, Whittingham, Vermont, January 24, 1913, Anderson Collection, LDS Church History Library, Salt Lake City, Utah.

Joseph Sr. did not know it, but he had lost his gamble with the weather even before he made it. A year earlier, Mount Tambora—a volcano on the island of Sumbawa in Indonesia, ten thousand miles away—had blown its top, sending twelve or more cubic miles of gas, ash, and dust as high as twenty-five miles into the atmosphere. By the summer of 1816, a haze of ash, dust, and sulfuric acid aerosol had encircled the earth, blocking sunlight. Temperatures plummeted, resulting in the famous "year without a summer" in 1816. Snow fell on parts of Virginia on the Fourth of July that year, and crops failed farther north and across much of Europe and Great Britain, leading to widespread famine and epidemics.[11] The Smiths' crops failed with all the rest.

True to his word, Joseph Sr. settled his debts and left for Palmyra, New York, later sending a team and wagon back for the family. Young Joseph had barely gotten off his crutches when Lucy and the children left Norwich—and Vermont—joining "ten to fifteen thousand others" who left the state over the course of the next two years in search of better prospects in warmer climes.[12]

3

New York and Pennsylvania

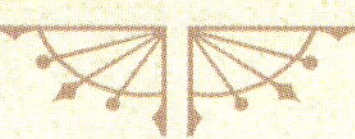

With such landmark events as the First Vision, Joseph's obtaining the golden plates, the translation and printing of the Book of Mormon, the restoration of the priesthood, and the organization of the Church taking place within their borders, one might legitimately refer to New York and Pennsylvania as the cradle of the Restoration. These two states also witnessed some of the more trying moments for Joseph and his family, such as the loss of the 116 pages of Book of Mormon manuscript, the death of Alvin, and the ultimate loss—again—of the family's land. By the time the Lord commanded the Saints to move to Ohio, however, perseverance, faith, revelation, and the ministry of angels had combined to begin to lay a sure foundation for the restored Church.

Joseph was just turning eleven when he and his family moved to the village of Palmyra. In 1818 or 1819, the family moved from Palmyra to a "snug log-house, neatly furnished," on a hundred-acre "farm" of uncleared land in Farmington (later Manchester) Township, just south of the Palmyra-Farmington Township line on Stafford Road.[1] Here Joseph was living when, at age fourteen, he received the First Vision. The log house was no longer standing when Anderson visited the site in August 1907 (two months after Elder George Albert Smith of the Quorum of the Twelve purchased the farm), but the very trees in the grove where God the Father and Jesus Christ appeared to Joseph were still there. Anderson took several photographs of the area, including shots from within the grove itself. Twelve-year-old Hugh Austin, the son of the farmer working the ground at the time, provided a sense of scale.

Young Joseph was just turning eleven when he and his family moved to the village of Palmyra.

The significance of the First Vision for Latter-day Saints—indeed, for the whole world—can hardly be overstated, and the Sacred Grove where it took place is one of the most important sites in Church history. Here Joseph went "on the morning of a beautiful, clear day, early in the spring of eighteen hundred and twenty" (Joseph Smith–History 1:14), seeking a remission of his sins (see D&C 20:5) and to ask God which church he should join. The question regarding forgiveness of his sins had been plaguing him for two years, and his decision to ask it in this particular grove of trees, where he had been chopping wood earlier, was apparently a deliberate

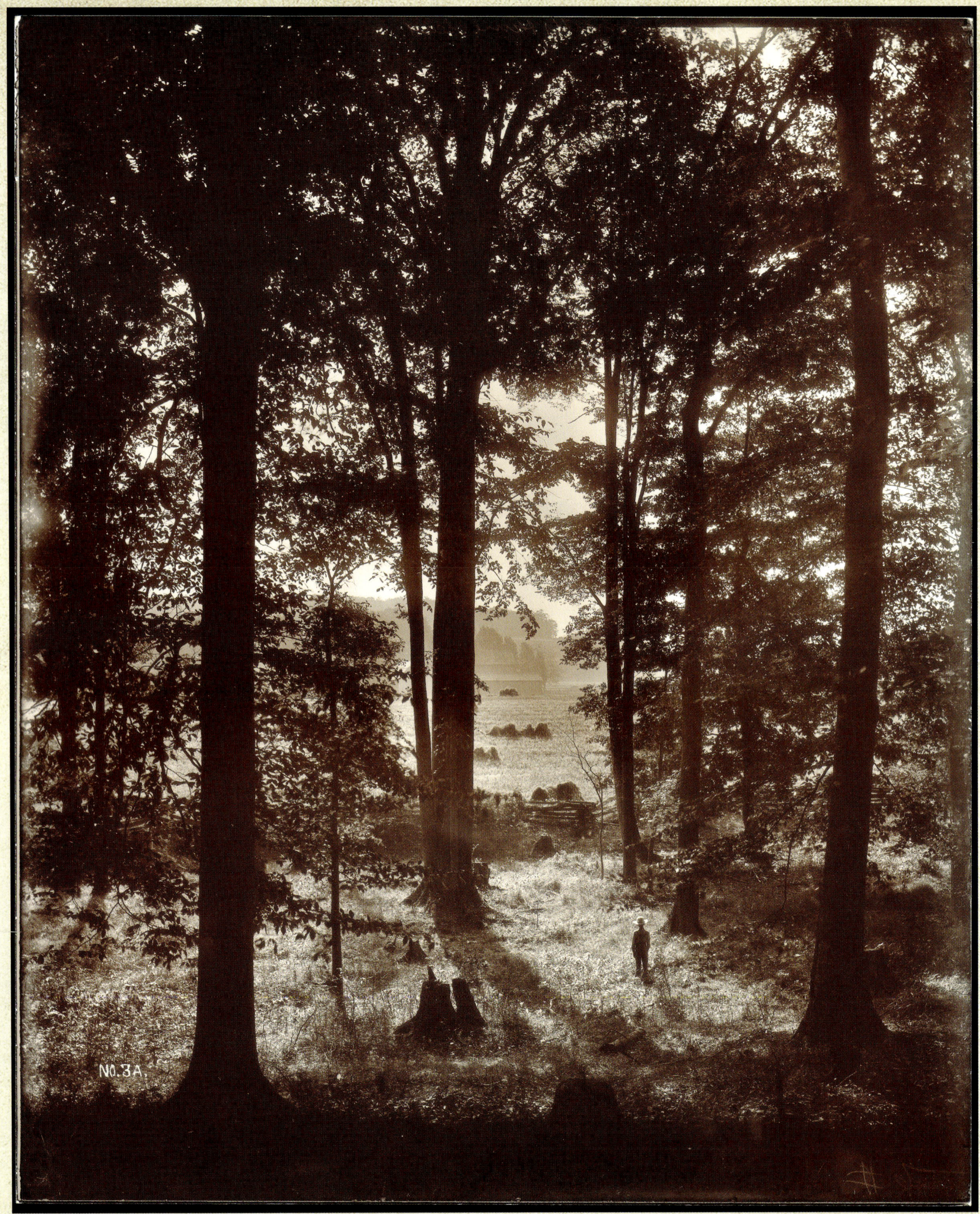

The Sacred Grove, Manchester, New York, August 13, 1907, Anderson Collection, LDS Church History Library, Salt Lake City, Utah.

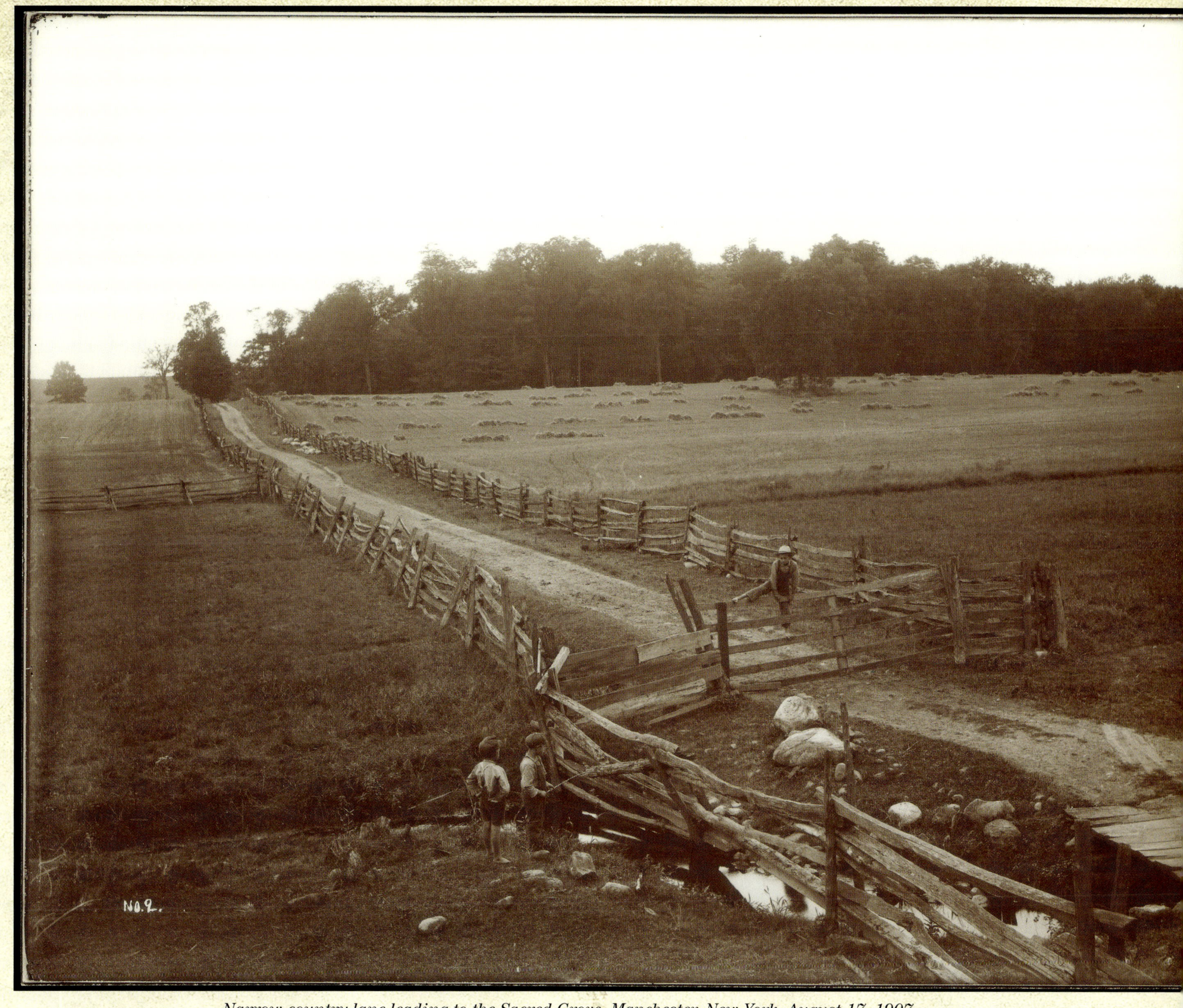

Narrow country lane leading to the Sacred Grove, Manchester, New York, August 17, 1907, Anderson Collection, LDS Church History Library, Salt Lake City, Utah.

one. The answer he received here—that his sins were forgiven him[2] but that he must join none of the existing churches—ushered in the dispensation of the fulness of times and laid the groundwork for the restoration of the gospel to the earth in the latter days.

The event's transcendent importance is perhaps best explained by President Gordon B. Hinckley: "Our entire case as members of The Church of Jesus Christ of Latter-day Saints rests on the validity of this glorious First Vision. It was the parting of the curtain to open this, the dispensation of the fulness of times. Nothing on which we base our doctrine, nothing we teach, nothing we live by is of greater importance than this initial declaration. I submit that if Joseph Smith talked with God the Father and His Beloved Son, then all else of which he spoke is true. This is the hinge on which turns the gate that leads to the path of salvation and eternal life."[3]

Anderson also took a picture of three boys fishing in Hathaway Brook next to the country lane that led west from the Smiths' log house to the Sacred Grove. Not only did this stream provide water for the Smith farm but it also may have been dammed to serve as a site for early baptisms.[4] Presumably, the grain field in Anderson's photograph was part of the sixty acres the Smith family cleared during their tenure on the farm, while the Sacred Grove itself was part of the forty acres of forest they left standing for a woodlot.[5] On the night of September 21, 1823, three and a half years after the First Vision, Joseph was visited by the angel Moroni, the last of a long line of prophets who had lived on the American continent in ancient times. Through Moroni, Joseph learned of the existence of a sacred record containing "an account of the former inhabitants of this continent" (Joseph Smith–History 1:34), which was hidden in a nearby hill—a drumlin left by retreating glaciers at the end of the last ice age. Deposited with the record was the means of translating it—"two stones in silver bows," which, when "fastened to a breastplate, constituted what is called the Urim and Thummim" (Joseph Smith–History 1:35). Joseph wrote later, "While he was thus conversing with me about the plates, the vision was opened to my mind that I could see the place where the plates were deposited, and that so clearly and distinctly that I knew the place again when I visited it" (Joseph Smith–History 1:42).

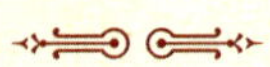

The Hill Cumorah has undergone considerable change over the past 190 years; however, it appears that the hill had changed little by the time Anderson photographed it in August 1907.

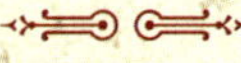

The hill where the plates were hidden lay in Manchester Township, three miles south of Joseph's log home on the hundred-acre farm. Following Moroni's instructions, and with his father's encouragement, seventeen-year-old Joseph visited the hill the following day. There, on the hill's north end—the end that appears in Anderson's photograph—and on the west side, "not far from the top, under a stone of considerable size" (Joseph Smith–History 1:51), Joseph found the plates, along with the Urim and Thummim and the breastplate. Forbidden by Moroni to remove them, Joseph was told to return to the hill to meet with the angel "precisely in one year from that time" and that he "should continue to do so until the time should come for obtaining the plates" (Joseph Smith–History 1:53). Joseph kept the yearly appointment on the hill—the Hill Cumorah, as it came to be called—for the next four years until Moroni delivered the plates to Joseph in the predawn hours of September 22, 1827.

Landscaped, fitted with props for the pageant that bears its name, and with a large statue of Moroni on its top today, the Hill Cumorah has undergone considerable change over the past 190 years. From Oliver Cowdery's 1835 description of the hill, however, it appears that the hill had changed little by the time Anderson photographed it in August 1907:

"The hill of which I have been speaking, at the time mentioned [1823], presented a varied appearance: The north end rose suddenly from the plain, forming a promontory without timber, but covered with grass. As you passed to the south you soon came to scattering timber, the surface having been cleared by art or by wind. . . . It is necessary to observe, that even the part cleared was only occupied for pasturage, its steep

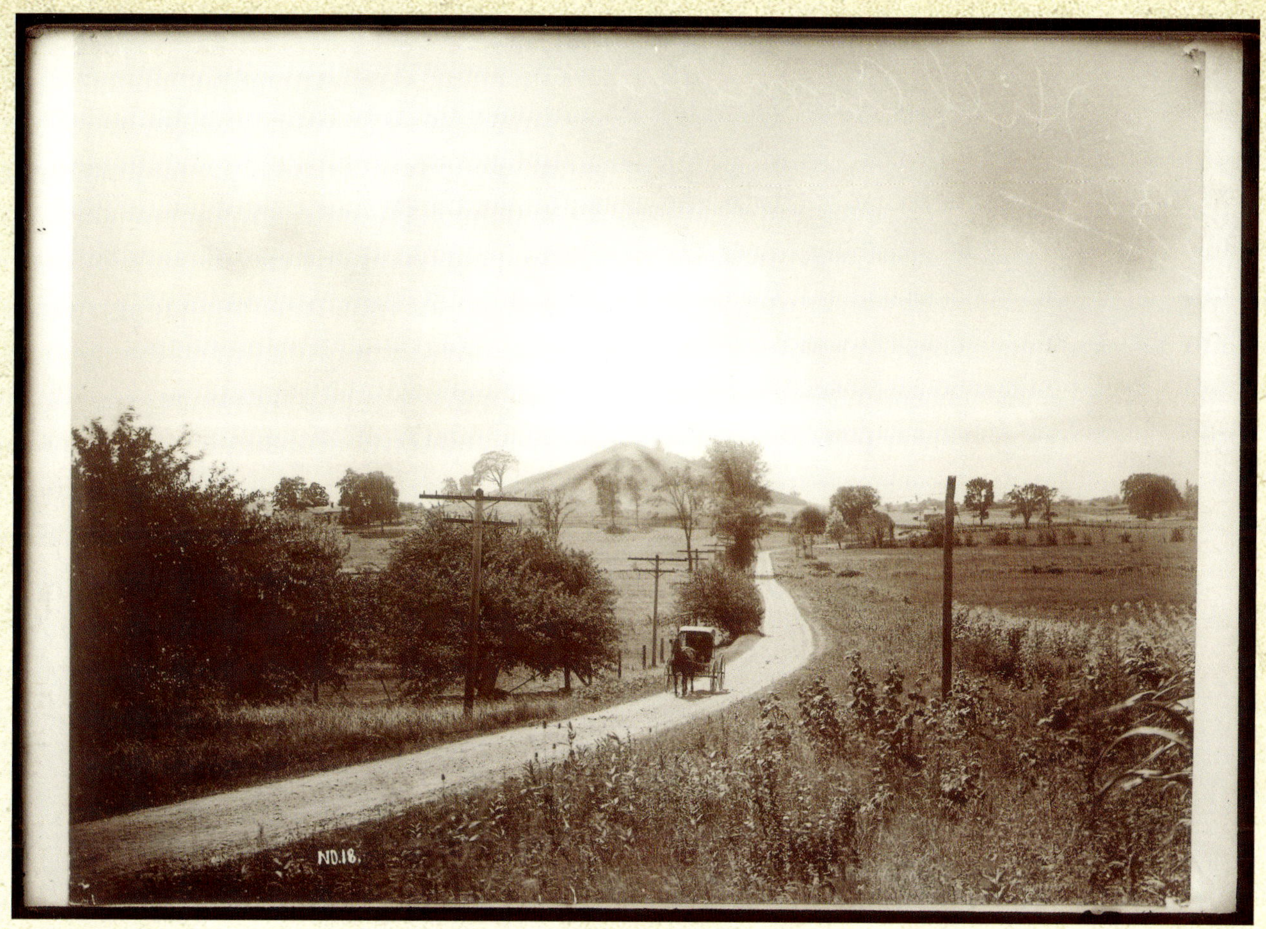

Hill Cumorah, Manchester, New York, August 1907, Anderson Collection, LDS Church History Library, Salt Lake City, Utah.

ascent and narrow summit not admitting the plow of the husbandman, with any degree of ease or profit. . . . When myself visited the place in the year 1830, there were several trees standing: enough to cause a shade in summer, but not so much as to prevent the surface from being covered with grass—which was also the case when the record was first found."[6]

It was Oliver's understanding as well that all of the records of the Nephites—not just the Book of Mormon—were deposited in this hill and that in a "beautiful vale" just to the west of the hill "the entire power and national strength of both the Jaredites and Nephites were destroyed."[7]

Many changes took place in Joseph's life and in the lives of members of his family between the time he first viewed the plates in 1823 and the time he finally obtained them in 1827. For one, the Smiths lost their farm in 1825 when they were unable to make the last mortgage payment on time. At the same time, they moved from the log home on the west side of Stafford Road to a frame home on the east side, where they resided as tenant farmers until the spring of 1829. Framed under the direction of Alvin Smith in 1822, the home was completed in late 1825 or early 1826 under the direction of Russell Stoddard after Alvin's death in November 1823. It was to this home, then—rather than the log home—that Joseph brought the plates in September 1827, "altogether speechless from fright and the fatigue of running" from three men who had attacked him on the way home.[8]

By the time Joseph obtained the plates, he was married to Emma Hale. The two had met in October 1825 in Harmony, Pennsylvania, when Joseph had boarded with the Hales family while working for Josiah Stowell. Suspicious of Joseph's religious experiences, Emma's father, Isaac Hale, opposed his daughter's budding romance with Joseph. Unable to obtain

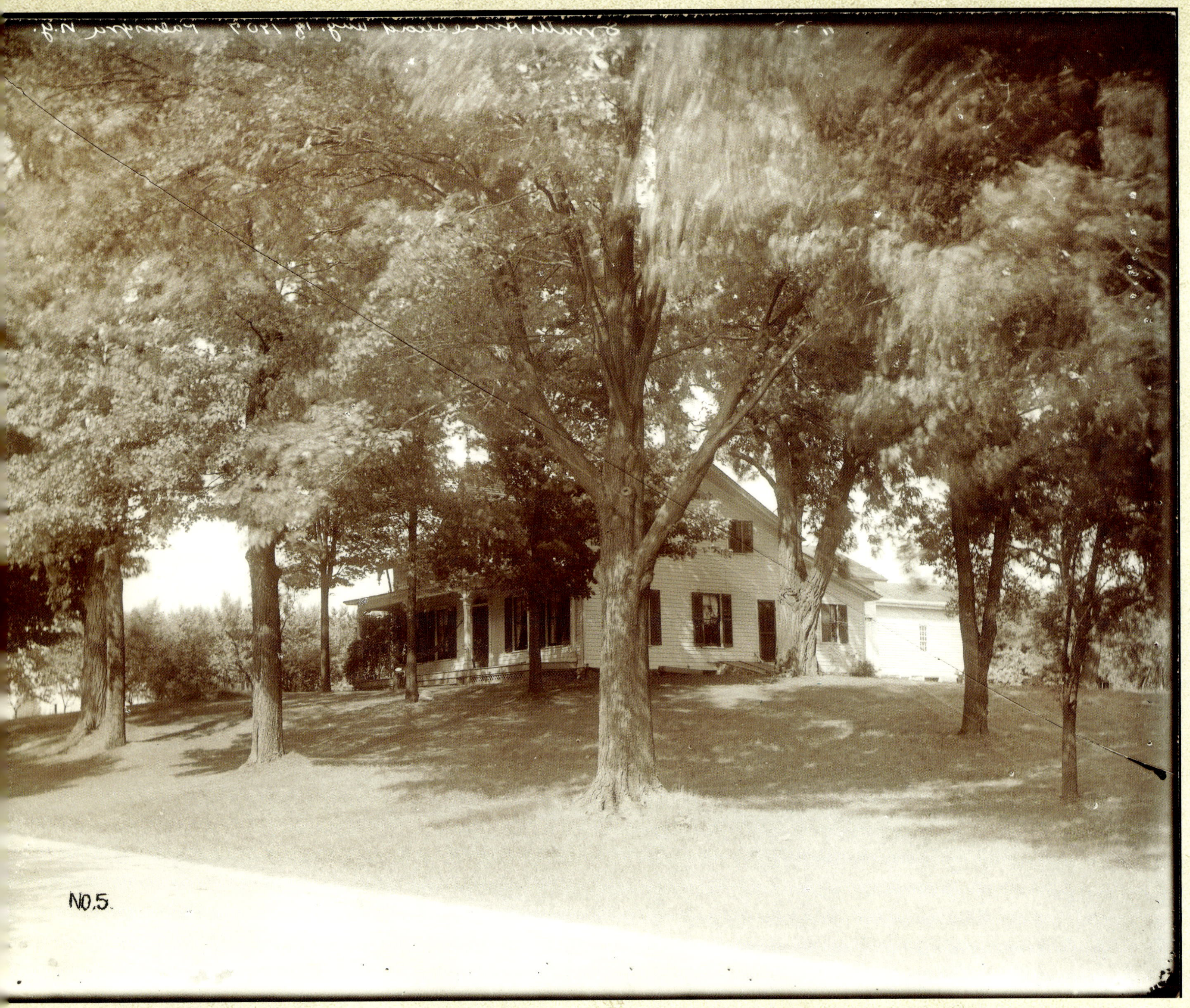

Frame home of Joseph and Lucy Mack Smith, Manchester, New York, August 19, 1907, Anderson Collection, LDS Church History Library, Salt Lake City, Utah.

Isaac's blessing, Joseph and Emma eloped on January 18, 1827, and moved into the frame home with Joseph's family in Manchester, where Joseph farmed with his father during the summer of 1827.

Despite its comfortable appearance, the frame home was anything but peaceful for the Smiths after Joseph received the plates. Word quickly spread that Joseph had the plates in his possession, and numbers of people, some offering "money and

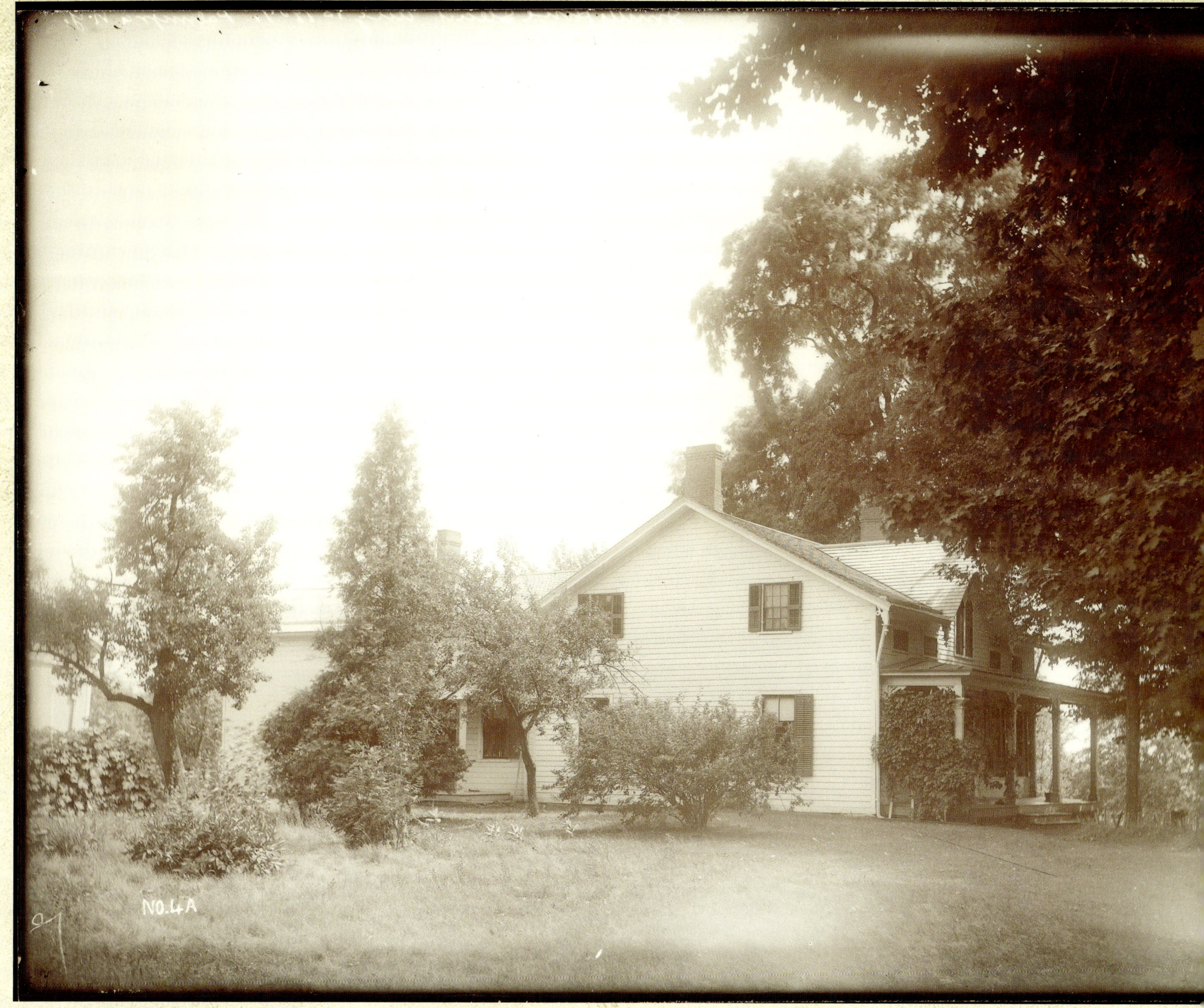

Frame home of Joseph and Lucy Mack Smith, Manchester, New York, August 19, 1907, Anderson Collection, LDS Church History Library, Salt Lake City, Utah.

property" to sweeten their offer, dropped by in hopes of seeing them. Joseph refused, of course, for which he and his family were "persecuted and abused." It was under these conditions that Joseph rushed into the house one day and asked his mother if "a company of men" had been by in his absence. When his mother told him that no one had come, he told her that "a mob would be there that night, if not before, to search for the record, and that it must be removed immediately." With the help of a trusted neighbor, Joseph "carefully and speedily" removed part of the hearth in the west room, buried the plates and the breastplate in a box, and reset the hearth over the box. Moments later, "a large company of armed men came rushing up to the house," at which Joseph opened the door and called out "as if he had a legion at hand, giving the word of command with great importance." He, his father, eleven-year-old Don Carlos, and perhaps others rushed outside toward the mob at the same time. The bluff worked, and the mob "fled . . . away into the woods, where they dispersed themselves to their several homes."[9]

Not long afterward, according to Joseph Knight, neighbor Samuel Lawrence and one "Beeman a great Rodsman" showed up at the home. When Joseph took them into the west room (where the plates were hidden under the hearth), they "proposed to go shares with him and tried every way" to get Joseph to share the plates with them. When Joseph refused, Beeman reportedly "took out his Rods and held them up and they pointed Down to the hearth where they were hid," at the same time exclaiming that he had found them. The two men apparently left without further ado, but when Joseph received "another intimation of the approach of a mob" a few days later, he dug the plates up from their hiding place in the house and buried them under his father's cooper shop across the road. With the frame home "frequently beset by mobs and evil designing persons" intent on getting the record, Joseph finally concluded to quit the Palmyra area for Harmony, Pennsylvania, where Emma's parents lived.[10]

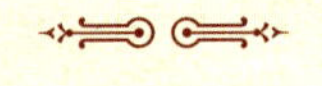

Despite its comfortable appearance, the frame home was anything but peaceful for the Smiths after Joseph received the plates.

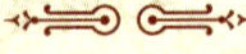

Joseph and Emma had planned to move in with the Hales family, but when Isaac insisted that he be allowed to see the plates, the couple moved to a small house built by Emma's brother Jesse. Here, away from the gaze of Emma's father and the mobs of Palmyra, Joseph finally had a chance to begin translating the plates. By February 1828, he reported, he had "copied a considerable number" of the characters from the plates "and by means of the Urim and Thummim . . . [had] translated some of them" (Joseph Smith–History 1:62).

At this point, Martin Harris visited Joseph and Emma in their little home in Harmony and reported that "the Lord had shown him that he must go to New York City with some of the characters." Joseph wrote, "We proceeded to copy some of them."[11] Afterward, Martin took, with Joseph's blessing, "the characters which had been translated, with the translation thereof, to Professor Charles Anthon, a gentleman celebrated for his literary attainments" (Joseph Smith–History 1:64). Anthon's subsequent request to have the book brought to him and his disappointment at learning that the book was sealed fulfilled prophecies contained in Isaiah 29:11–12 and 2 Nephi 27:6–10, 15–20.

Martin was back in Harmony on April 12, when he began serving as Joseph's scribe while Joseph translated the plates. By June 14, the manuscript Martin had written numbered 116 pages. The well-known story of Martin's subsequent loss of these pages constituted only one of the tragedies that struck Joseph and Emma in their little house in Harmony that summer. On June 15, the day after Martin left for Palmyra with the 116 pages, Emma gave birth to her first child, a boy, who was named Alvin and who died the same day. Joseph buried his son in a little cemetery nearby, the grave's headstone still clearly legible when Anderson visited the area almost

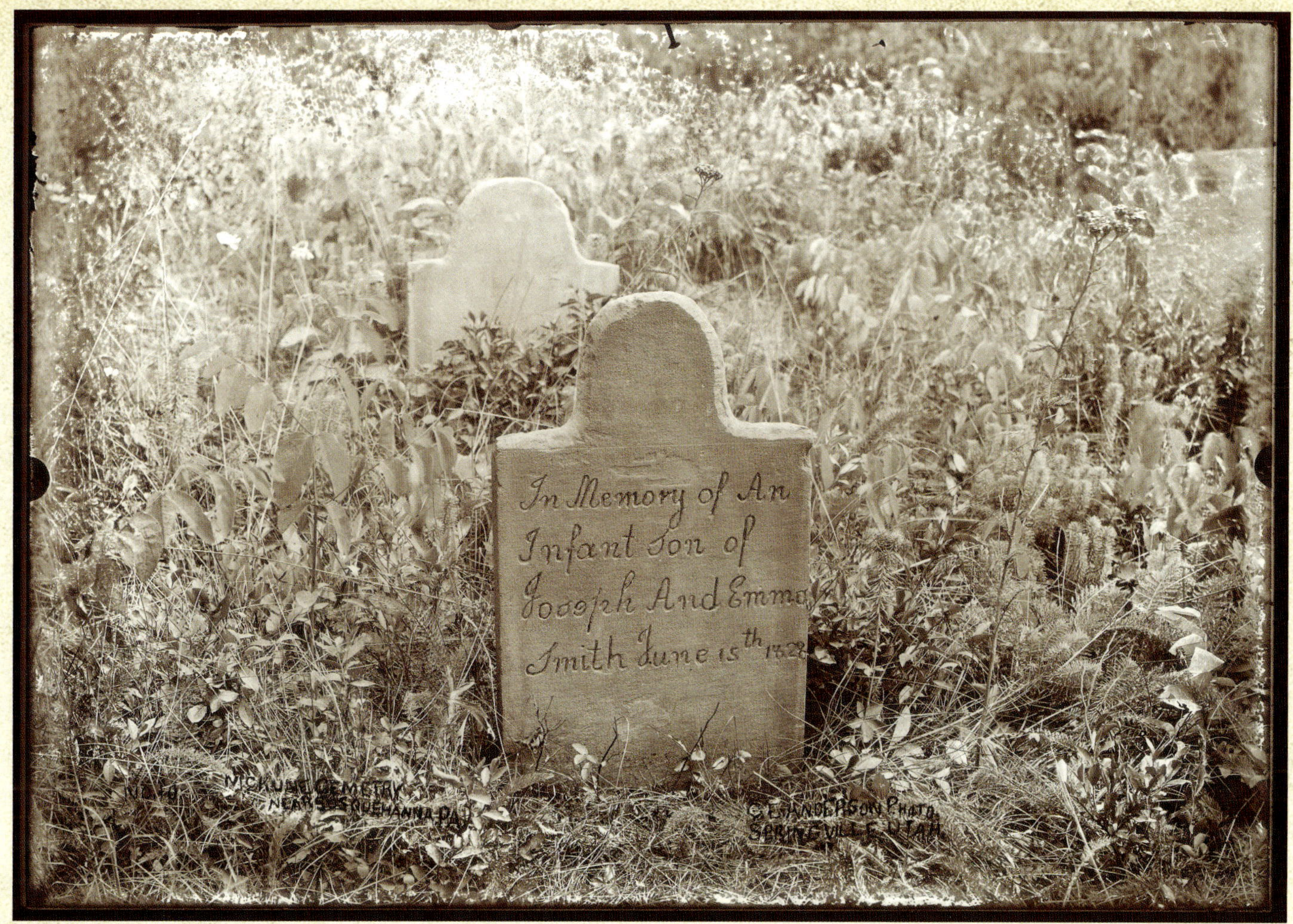

Tombstone of Alvin Smith, Joseph and Emma Smith's firstborn son, Harmony, Pennsylvania, 1907, Anderson Collection, LDS Church History Library, Salt Lake City, Utah.

eighty years later. Emma's health failed for a time as well, and for two weeks Joseph stayed by her side and nursed her back to health.

When Emma had recovered sufficiently, Joseph left Harmony for Palmyra, where he learned that Martin had lost the 116 pages he had taken. Immediately upon his return to Harmony, Joseph recorded later, "the former heavenly messenger [Moroni] appeared and handed to me the Urim and Thummim again (for it had been taken from me in consequence of my having wearied the Lord in asking for the privilege of letting Martin Harris take the writings)." Through the Urim and Thummim, Joseph learned that he had lost the privilege of translating for a time, a privilege that would be restored only on the condition of repentance. Moroni then took possession both of the plates and of the Urim and Thummim.[12]

By the end of the summer—Lucy says it was on September 22[13]—Joseph had received the plates and the Urim and Thummim again, with the charge not to retranslate the material he had lost. Joseph could do little, however, without a full-time scribe. Emma helped when she could, and Joseph's brother Samuel reportedly wrote a little, but the plates and the instrument probably spent a good part of the following winter in the "red morocco trunk, lying on Emma's bureau," where Joseph kept them.[14] Joseph was in good spirits when his mother and father visited him in Harmony in February 1829, but by early April he was pleading to the Lord for a scribe. Informed that one "should be forthcoming in a few days," Joseph was "not at all surprised" when Oliver Cowdery showed up at his doorstep on April 5.[15]

Oliver had heard about—and prayed about—the gold

plates while teaching school in Palmyra the previous winter and had become "so completely absorbed in the subject of the Record," according to Lucy, "that it seemed impossible for him to think or converse about anything else."[16] Work on the translation began in earnest with Oliver's arrival in Harmony, transforming Joseph and Emma's house into a scriptorium, that is, a place dedicated to copying and producing sacred texts.

"Day after day I continued," Oliver wrote later, "uninterrupted, to write from his [Joseph's] mouth, as he translated with the Urim and Thummim . . . the history, or record, called 'the book of Mormon.'"[17] Progress was particularly rapid, thanks to the help of Joseph Knight, who owned a farm in Colesville, New York, about thirty miles up the Susquehanna River from Harmony. A friend of the Smith family, Knight "very kindly and considerately brought us, a quantity of provisions, in order that we might not be interrupted in the work of translation, by the want of such necessaries of life," Joseph wrote. Knight's willingness to do this "several times . . . enabled us to continue the work when otherwise we must have relinquished it for a season."[18]

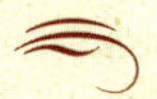

Along with translating the plates, Joseph received several revelations in his home in Harmony during this time. Topics ranged from instructions to Oliver about his specific spiritual gifts to the fate of the apostle John (see D&C 6–9; 11–12). The translation itself prompted inquiries into other topics as well, which led to further revelations. On May 15, for example, after "writing the account given of the Savior's ministry" to the Nephites in the Book of Mormon, Joseph and Oliver walked down the hill from the house to the banks of the Susquehanna to "inquire of the Lord respecting baptism for the remission of sins, that we found mentioned in the translation of the plates" (Joseph Smith–History 1:71n, 68).

Joseph was "not at all surprised" when Oliver Cowdery showed up at his doorstep on April 5, 1829.

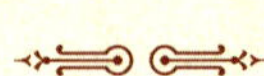

While they were praying, an angel identifying himself as "John, the same that is called John the Baptist in the New Testament" appeared and ordained Joseph and Oliver to the Aaronic Priesthood, "which holds the keys of . . . baptism by immersion for the remission of sins" (Joseph Smith–History 1:72; D&C 13:1). Following the angel's instructions, Joseph then baptized Oliver and Oliver baptized Joseph, after which Joseph ordained Oliver to the Aaronic Priesthood and Oliver ordained Joseph—"for so we were commanded," the Prophet wrote (Joseph Smith–History 1:71). Ten days later, after "much enquiry and explanation," Oliver baptized Joseph's younger brother Samuel.[19]

The banks of the Susquehanna served as the site for the restoration of the Melchizedek Priesthood as well. Shortly after John the Baptist's visitation and the restoration of the Aaronic Priesthood—probably within two weeks—the ancient apostles Peter, James, and John appeared to Joseph and Oliver somewhere "in the wilderness" (D&C 128:20) between Harmony and Colesville and ordained them to the Melchizedek Priesthood, which "holds the right of presidency, and has power and authority over all the offices in the church in all ages of the world, to administer in spiritual things" (D&C 107:8).

According to Addison Everett, who reported in 1882 that he had heard Joseph talk about the event several years later in Nauvoo, Joseph and Oliver at the time were fleeing from a mob that had formed in Colesville, where they had gone

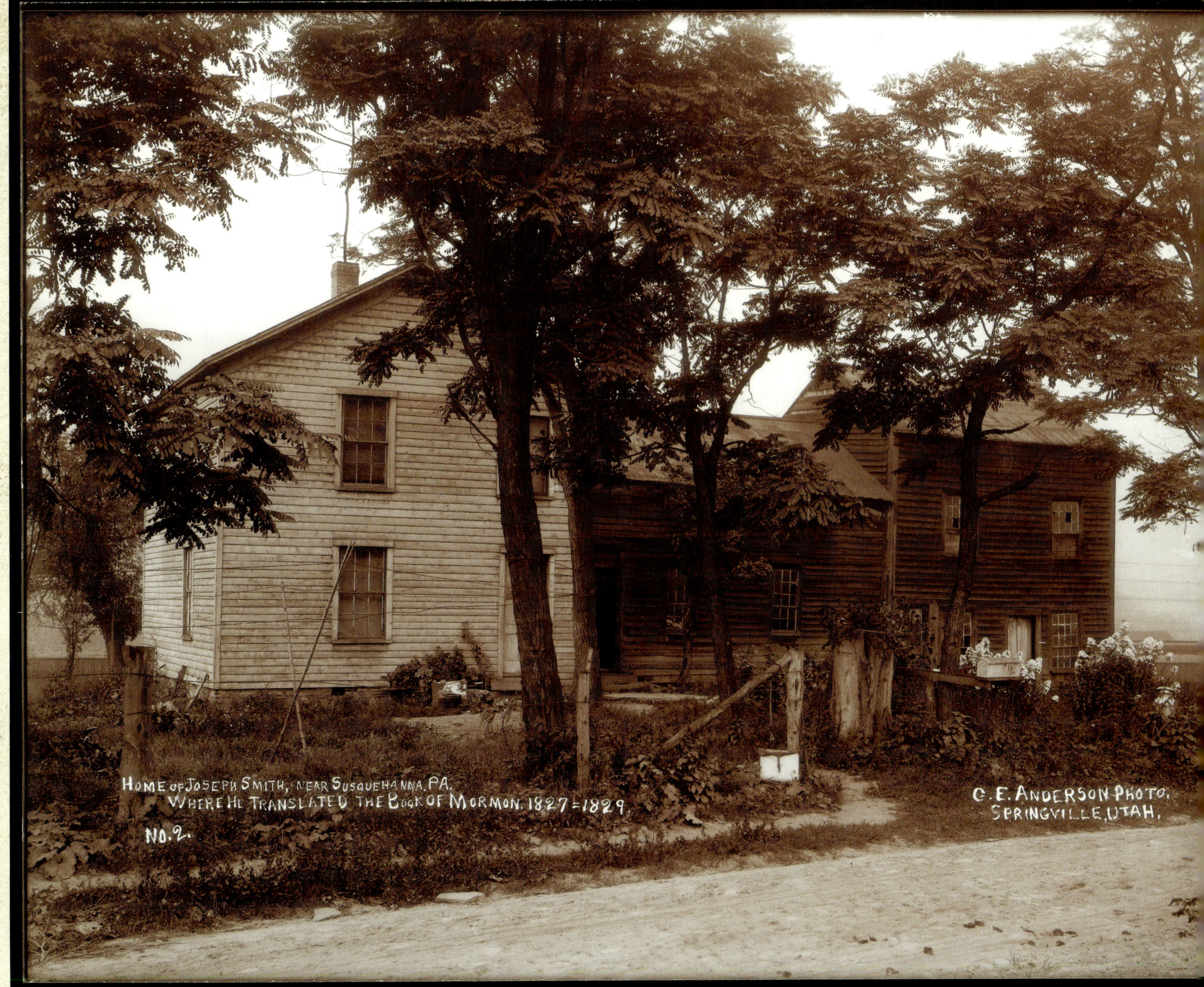

Home of Joseph and Emma Hale Smith (center frame structure is original Smith home), Harmony, Pennsylvania, 1907, Anderson Collection, LDS Church History Library, Salt Lake City, Utah.

to preach at the request of Joseph Knight. Everett recounted: "They wandered in a dense forest all night, and oftentimes in mud and water up to their knees. And Brother Oliver got quite exhausted in the after part of the night, and Brother Joseph had to put his arm around him and almost carry him. And just as the day broke in the east, Brother Oliver gave out entirely and he, Brother Joseph, leaned him against an oak tree just outside a field fence, Brother Oliver crying out, 'How long, O Lord, O how long, Brother Joseph, have we got to suffer these things?'" Everett quoted Joseph as saying then, "'Just this moment

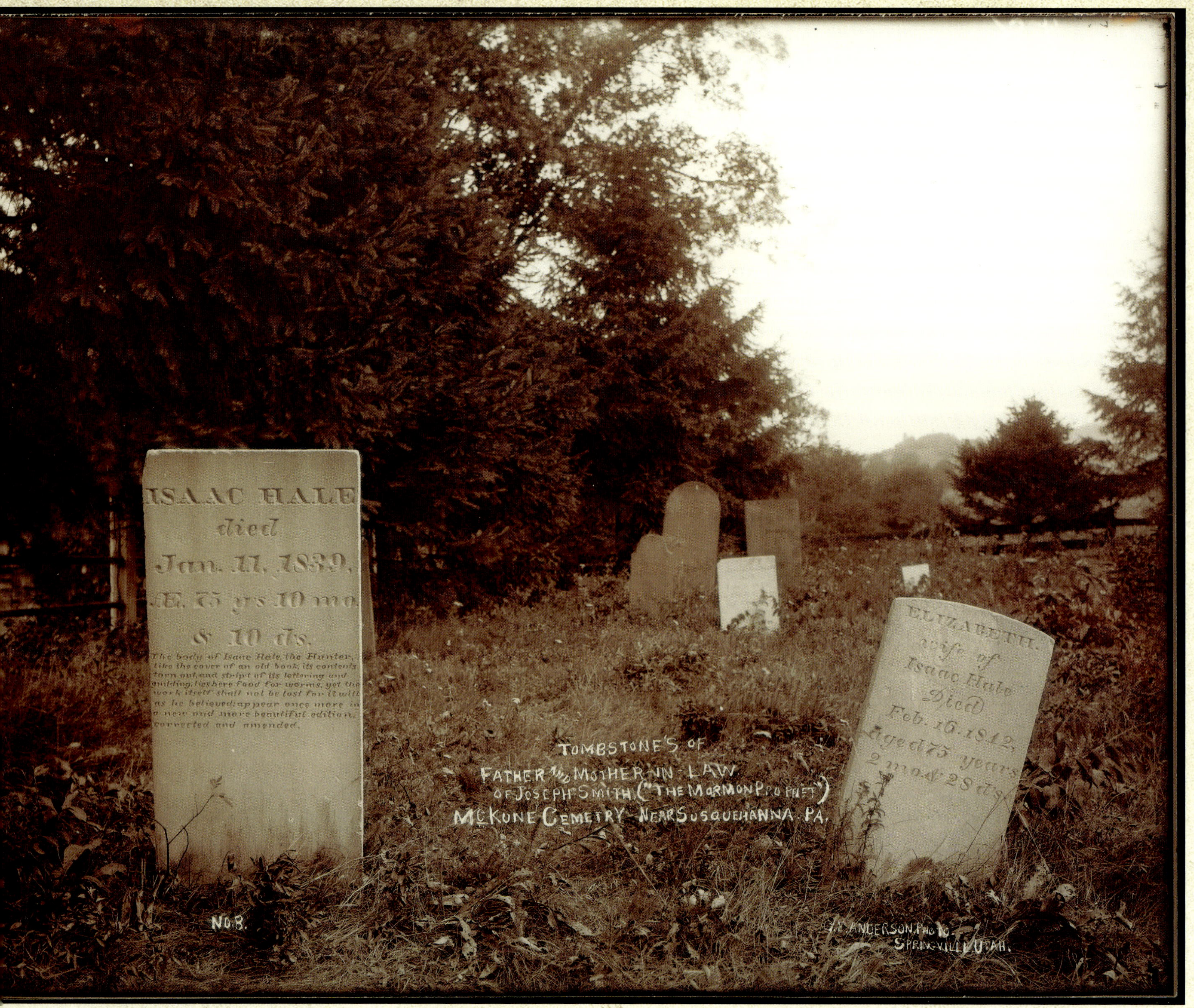

Tombstones of Isaac and Elizabeth Hale, Emma Hale Smith's mother and father, Harmony, Pennsylvania, 1907, Anderson Collection, LDS Church History Library, Salt Lake City, Utah.

Peter, James, and John came to us and ordained us to the Holy Apostleship and gave unto us the keys of the dispensation of the fulness of times. And we had some sixteen or seventeen miles to go to reach our place of residence.'"[20]

With many people in the Harmony-Colesville area becoming more and more antagonistic, Joseph wrote to Oliver's friend David Whitmer in Fayette, New York, "requesting him to come immediately with his team, and convey [Joseph] and Oliver to his own residence," where they could finish the translation in safety.[21] David complied, proposing upon his arrival in

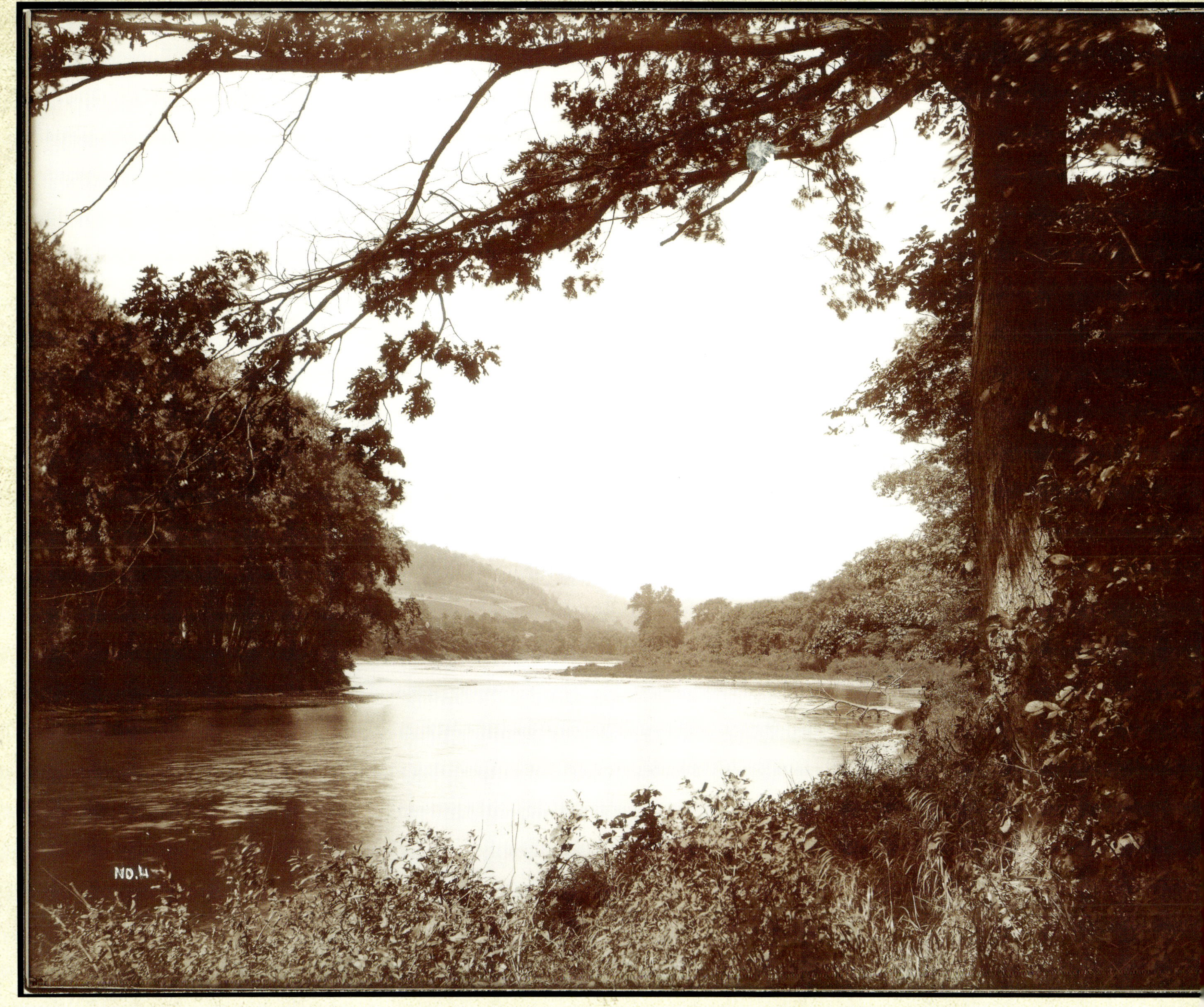

Susquehanna River, Harmony, Pennsylvania, 1907, Anderson Collection, LDS Church History Library, Salt Lake City, Utah.

Harmony that Joseph and Oliver live with the Whitmer family free of charge and that he or one of his brothers serve as a scribe if necessary.[22] By early June 1829, the three men and the plates were safely at David's father's house in Fayette—Joseph, Oliver, and David having traveled in David's two-horse wagon and the plates, apparently, having been conveyed by Moroni.[23] Emma remained in Harmony for a time.

The move to Fayette was a good one. The Whitmers' quiet farm—still fairly isolated in 1907, as Anderson's photograph shows—proved an excellent place to complete the translation, while David's brother John was able to assist Oliver significantly as scribe. David's whole family, in fact, were "very anxious concerning the work, and very friendly towards ourselves," Joseph wrote. So too were the people of Seneca County in general, many of whom were "disposed to enquire into the truth of these strange matters which now began to be noised abroad."[24] It was a very different reception from those Joseph had been accustomed to receiving and one that he took full advantage of: "Many opened their houses to us in order that we might have an opportunity of meeting with our friends for the purposes of instruction and explanation. We met with many from time to time, who were willing to hear us, and wishful to find out the truth as it is in Christ Jesus, and apparently willing to obey the Gospel when once fairly convinced and satisfied in their own minds." Many were baptized during this time, including David, his brother Peter, and Joseph's brother Hyrum.[25]

The Whitmer home, like the home in Harmony, served as the setting for several revelations unrelated to the translation of the plates. Several of these revelations involved instructions to various members of the Whitmer family, including David, John, and Peter Jr. (see D&C 14–16). All emphasized the importance of missionary work, including one given to David and Oliver appointing them to "search out" twelve men to receive the apostleship (D&C 18). It was also during this time, in "the Chamber of Mr Whitmer's house," that Joseph and Oliver received instructions to ordain each other to be elders but only after those who had been and would be baptized could assemble together and manifest their willingness to accept the two men as their "spiritual teachers."[26] This inaugurated, in effect, the law of common consent in the latter days and ratified their authority to use the Melchizedek Priesthood, which they had received earlier.

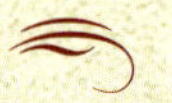

At least two important things had to happen before this sustaining vote could take place. Both involved the Book of Mormon. The first, as spelled out in the record itself, was that three men needed to view the plates "by the power of God" (2 Nephi 27:12; Ether 5:3). The second was the actual publication of the Book of Mormon.

Having learned of the need for three special witnesses, Oliver, David, and Martin Harris—who was visiting Fayette from Palmyra—asked Joseph if they might be the ones. An affirmative answer through the Urim and Thummim (D&C 17) sent Joseph and the other three men into "a piece of woods convenient to Mr Whitmer's house," where they knelt together and began taking turns praying for a view of the plates. After each man had prayed twice with no results, Martin Harris excused himself, apparently believing that his presence was the problem.

"Behold, an angel stood before us; in his hands he held the plates which we had been praying for these to have a view of."

"He accordingly withdrew from us," recorded Joseph, "and we knelt down again, and had not been many minutes engaged in prayer when presently we beheld a light above us in the air of exceeding brightness, and behold, an angel stood before us; in his hands he held the plates which we had been praying for these to have a view of." The angel allowed the men to see the engravings on the plates, after which a voice "from out of the bright light above" bore testimony to the truth of the translation and commanded the men to bear their own testimonies of what they were seeing and hearing. Leaving Oliver and David, Joseph then tracked down Martin Harris "at

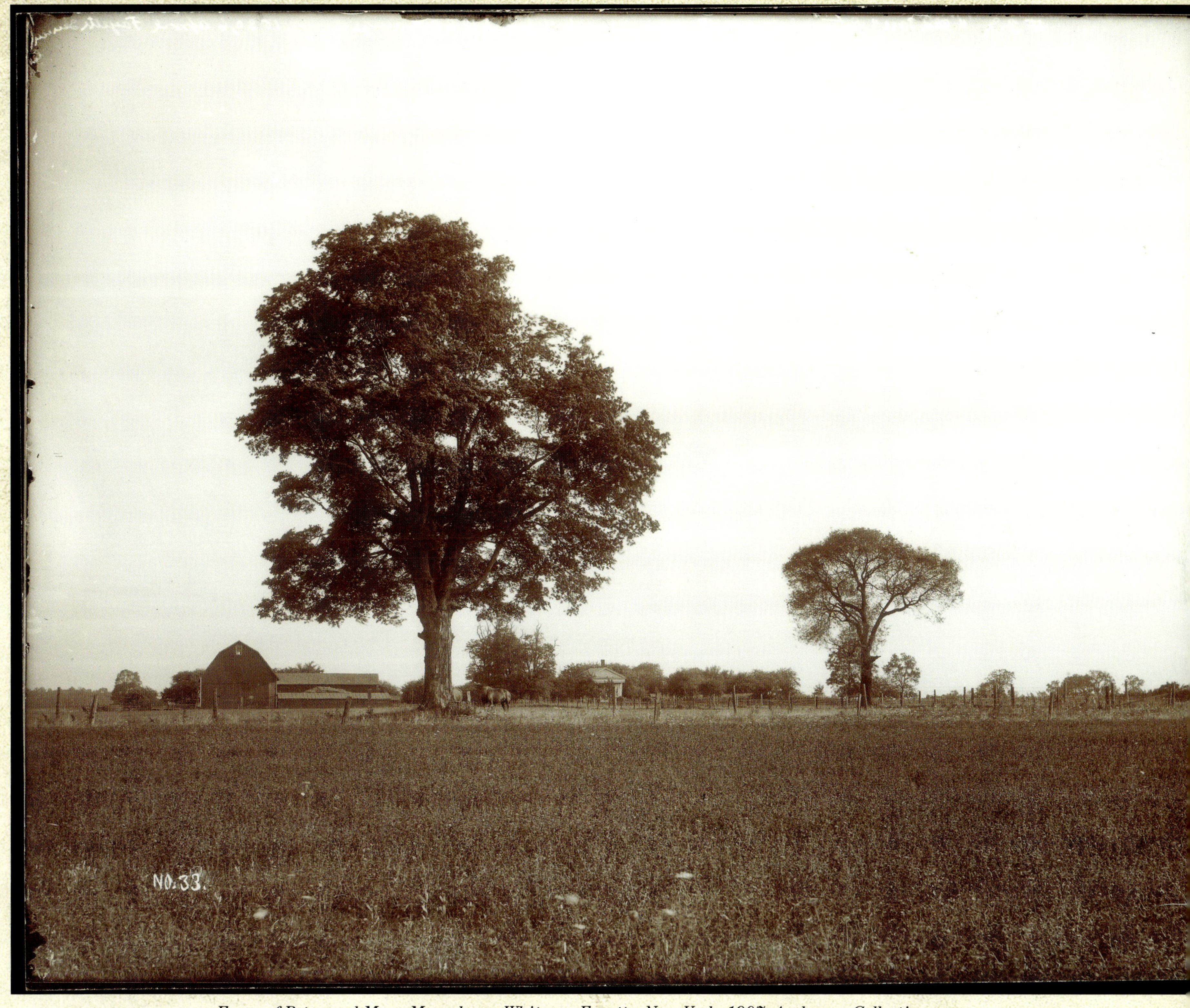

Farm of Peter and Mary Musselman Whitmer, Fayette, New York, 1907, Anderson Collection, LDS Church History Library, Salt Lake City, Utah.

a Considerable distance," and Martin ultimately received the same manifestation.[27]

The experience was almost too much for Martin, who jumped up, shouted "Hosanna," and "otherwise rejoiced exceedingly."[28] David and Oliver also reported that "no tongue could express the joy of their hearts, and the greatness of the things which they had both seen and heard."[29] According to Lucy, who was in Fayette on a visit at the time, the Three Witnesses were not the only ones thrilled at the experience. Returning to the Whitmer home sometime between three and four in the afternoon, Joseph "threw himself down" beside his mother, who was sitting in a bedroom with Joseph Sr. and Mrs. Whitmer.

"Father, mother," Joseph exclaimed, "you do not know how happy I am; the Lord has now caused the plates to be shown to three more besides myself. . . . They will have to bear witness to the truth of what I have said, for now they know for themselves, that I do not go about to deceive the people, and I feel as if I was relieved of a burden which was almost too heavy for me to bear, and it rejoices my soul, that I am not any longer to be entirely alone in the world."[30]

It was imperative now that the Book of Mormon be published. Accordingly, after finishing the translation at the Whitmer home, Joseph made his way back to Palmyra, where he contracted with E. B. Grandin, owner and editor of the *Wayne Sentinel,* to print five thousand copies of the Book of Mormon for three thousand dollars. The contract had not been easy to secure: Grandin had initially refused the job, as had Thurlow Weed, a publisher in Rochester; Elihu Marshall, another publisher in Rochester, had accepted it, but his print shop was an inconvenient twenty miles from Joseph's home. Only after Martin Harris agreed to stand as security for the entire three thousand dollars did Grandin relent. Printing apparently commenced at the end of August 1829 on the third floor of Grandin's Bookstore in Palmyra, identified with a vertical "B M" in Anderson's photograph. The book was bound in Luther Howard's bindery on the second floor. Having several employees, Grandin was able to have the book ready for sale on March 26, 1830.

The printing of the Book of Mormon commenced at the end of August 1829 on the third floor of Grandin's Bookstore in Palmyra.

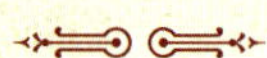

The printing process did not go without incident, though. Shortly after work had begun, one of the printers overheard a group of citizens in an adjoining room planning to steal the Book of Mormon manuscript from Lucy Smith, in whose care Joseph had left it for a time. Apprised of the situation by Oliver, who had been in the printing office at the time, Lucy was able to keep the manuscript out of harm's way.[31] Then one Sunday in December 1829, Hyrum and Oliver stumbled upon Abner Cole, a former justice of the peace, in Grandin's shop printing his weekly paper, the *Reflector.* After learning that Cole rented Grandin's press weeknights and Sundays, the two men were upset to find that he had been printing extracts from the Book of Mormon in his paper.

When Cole refused to desist in his "dishonest course," Joseph Sr. traveled to Harmony for Joseph. Arriving in Palmyra on a Sunday, Joseph found Cole hard at work on his paper in Grandin's shop. After "good naturedly" saluting the printer and examining his paper, Joseph reminded Cole of the copyright and insisted that he stop "meddling" with the Book of Mormon. At this, Cole reportedly "threw off his coat, rolled up his sleeves, and came towards Joseph, smacking his fists together with vengeance" and challenging the Prophet to a fight. Remaining calm and trying to defuse the situation, Joseph simply smiled at the display, refused the challenge, and suggested—given the wintry season—that the enraged man keep his coat on. Following another frenzied outburst, Joseph again reminded Cole of the copyright and the legal avenues that he, as copyright holder, could pursue that would serve his purposes far better than a brawl. Cole finally calmed down and "concluded to submit to an arbitration," which was decided in Joseph's favor.[32] Cole stopped publishing portions of the Book of Mormon as a result,

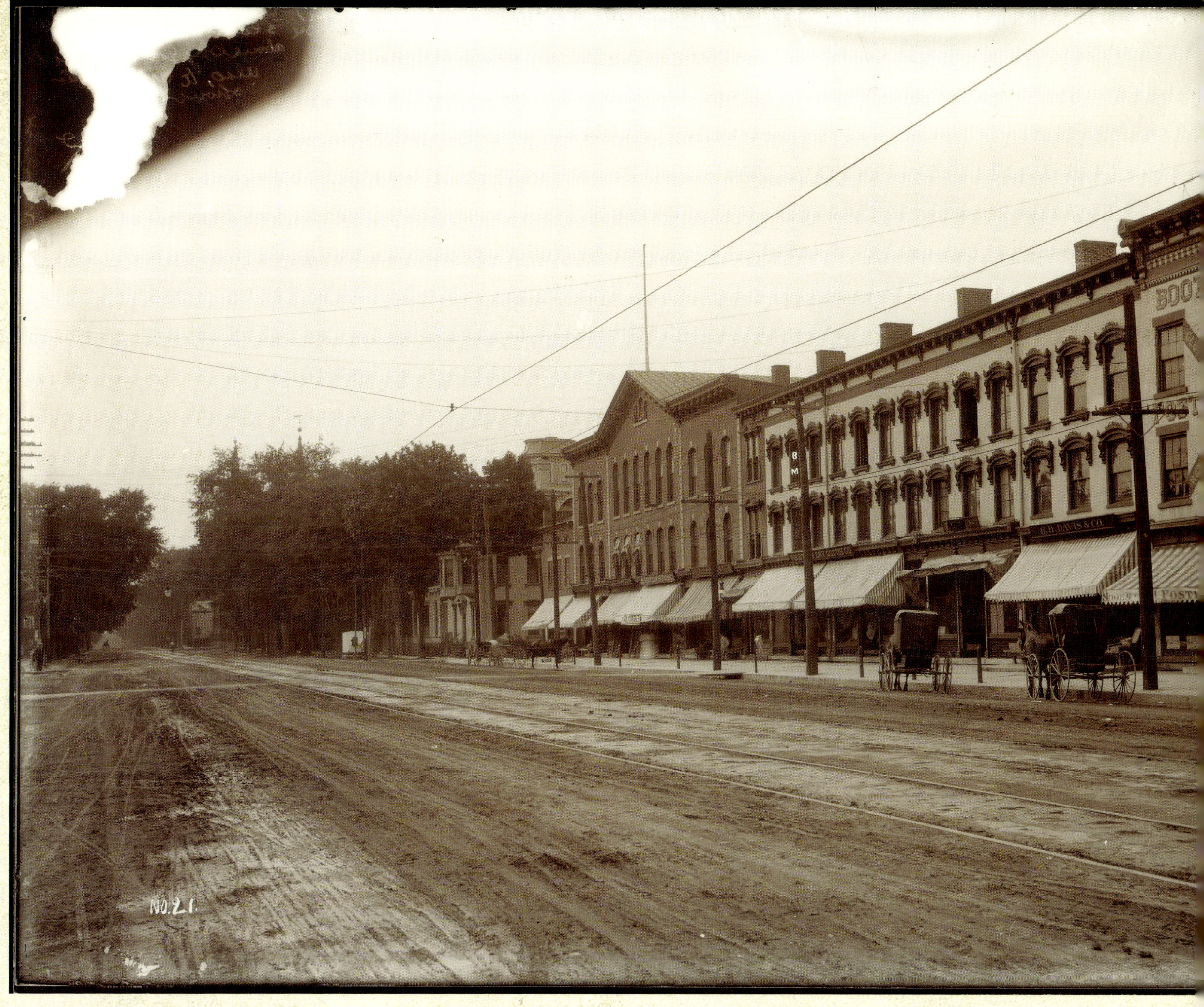

Main Street (Grandin Printing Office identified with "B" and "M" written vertically in third-story window), Palmyra, New York, August 1907, Anderson Collection, LDS Church History Library, Salt Lake City, Utah.

but for months afterward he continued to poke fun at Joseph and satirize the Book of Mormon in his paper—using the same press, ironically, on which the Book of Mormon was printed.

With the witnesses in place and the Book of Mormon published, the way was clear for Joseph and Oliver to be sustained as spiritual leaders and ordained as elders. All this was done on April 6, 1830, in conjunction with the official organization of the Church. On that day, approximately fifty people gathered at the Whitmer home in Fayette. In accordance with New York's 1813 "Act to provide for the Incorporation of

Religious Societies," which required a religious organization to be established by "not less than three, nor exceeding nine" men,[33] six of those present—Joseph Smith, Oliver Cowdery, David Whitmer, Hyrum Smith, Samuel Smith, and Peter Whitmer Jr.—constituted the original organization. These six voted to accept Joseph and Oliver as "their teachers in the things of the Kingdom of God" and to "be organized as a Church," after which Joseph and Oliver ordained each other elders in the Church. After receiving the sacrament, each man was confirmed a member of the Church and received the gift of the Holy Ghost.[34]

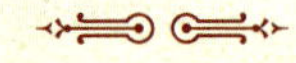

Colesville's idyllic setting masks the persecution that attended the rise of the Church in the area.

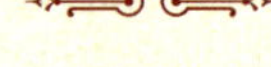

At the time of the organization of the Church, Joseph received the revelation now recorded as Doctrine and Covenants 21, in which his calling as "a seer, a translator, a prophet, an apostle of Jesus Christ, [and] an elder of the church" was confirmed, and in which the newly organized church was commanded to "give heed unto all his words and commandments . . . in all patience and faith" (D&C 21:1, 4–5). Five days later, on April 11, the members of the Church met again at the Whitmer home for their first Sunday meeting.[35]

Following the organization of the Church, Joseph divided his time between the Harmony and Colesville areas and Fayette. His labors in Colesville centered on the Joseph Knight family, whose members had contributed materially to the translation of the Book of Mormon. The "several meetings" Joseph held in the area were well attended, but it was not until perhaps eight or ten adults saw Joseph cast an evil spirit out of Joseph Knight's son Newel—an event Joseph referred to as the first miracle of the Church—that the Church gained a solid hold in

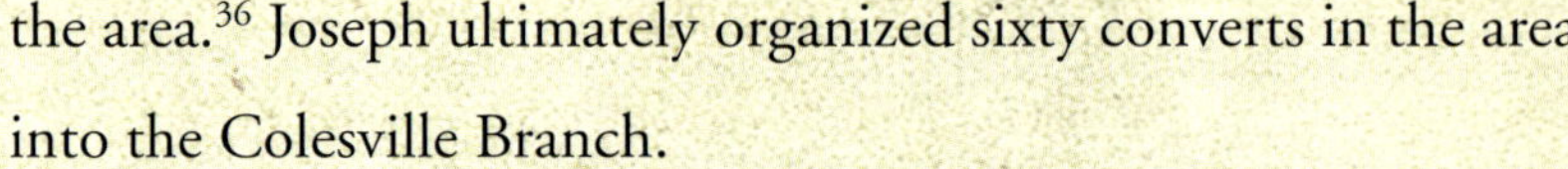

the area.[36] Joseph ultimately organized sixty converts in the area into the Colesville Branch.

Colesville's idyllic setting—captured beautifully in Anderson's photograph—masks the persecution that attended the rise of the Church in the area. Residents opposed to Joseph's teachings used everything from persuasion to intimidation to dissuade their neighbors from joining the Church, even tearing down a dam Joseph and others had constructed for baptisms. When these tactics failed, Abram W. Benton, a Presbyterian, swore out a warrant against Joseph, charging him with being a disorderly person. Joseph was arrested just as he was opening a confirmation meeting for those who had been baptized, narrowly escaping a mob as he was being conducted to a neighboring county for trial. When, after several hours, nothing could be sustained against him, Joseph's persecutors obtained another warrant from Broome County—where Colesville was located—and subjected him to another hours-long trial there. This too ended in Joseph's acquittal, after which he returned to his home in Harmony for safety. Another mob formed upon his and Oliver's arrival in Colesville several days later, forcing them to return downriver during the night. It was more than a month before he was able to return to Colesville and confirm those who had been baptized earlier.

Joseph made good use of his time in Harmony as he waited for things to calm down in Colesville. Along with working on his inspired translation of the Bible—a project that would soon yield the book of Moses found in today's Pearl of Great Price—he started to "arrange and copy" the revelations he had received.[37] He also received several important revelations, including one to Emma—the only revelation in the Doctrine

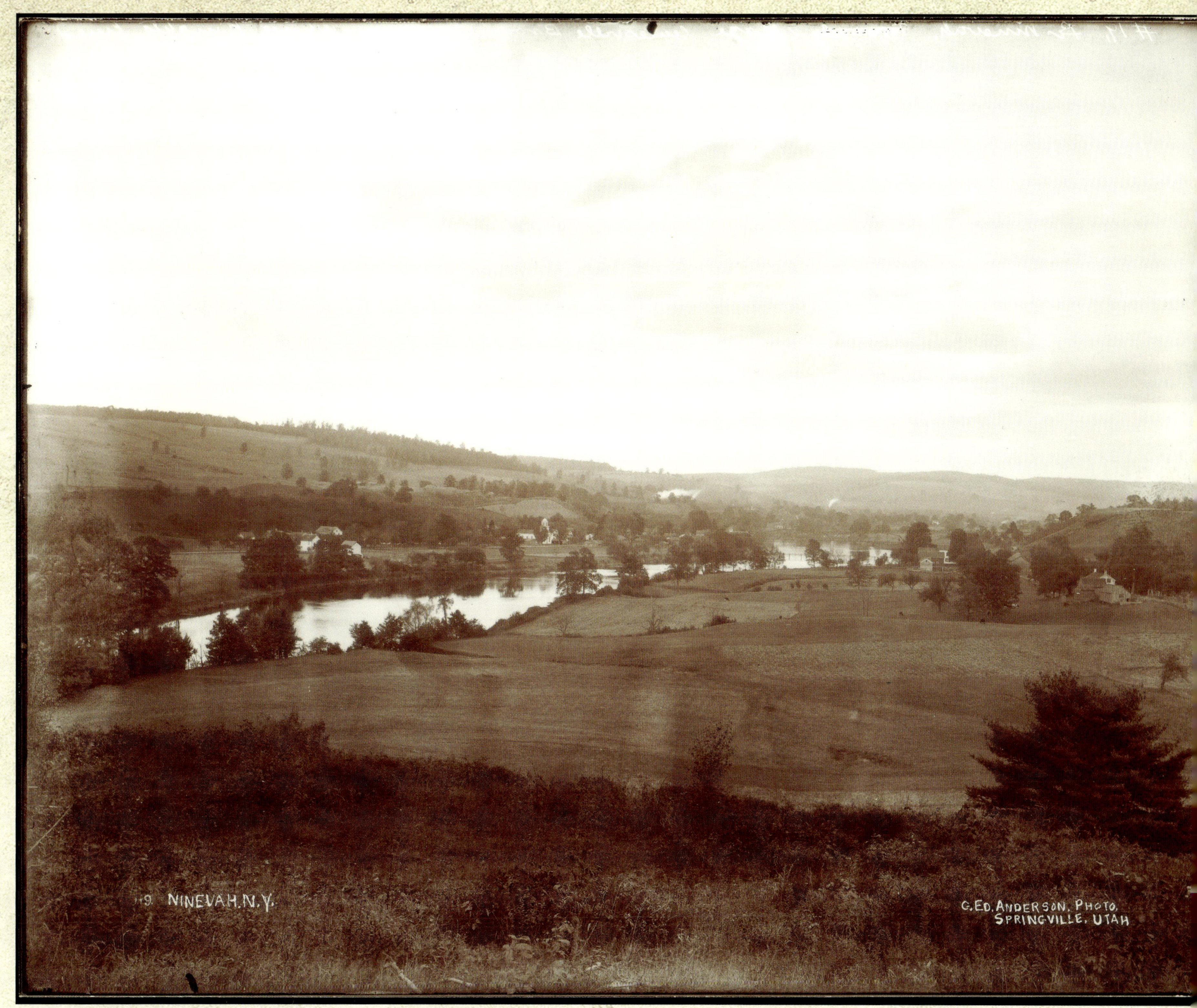

Location of the Colesville Branch, Nineveh, Broome County, New York, 1907, Anderson Collection, LDS Church History Library, Salt Lake City, Utah.

and Covenants devoted exclusively to a woman—and a revelation about the emblems of the sacrament (D&C 27).

By August, however, Harmony also had become a seat of increasing persecution against the Prophet. Much of it came about through the exertions of Emma's uncle Nathaniel Lewis, a devout Methodist who "went to visit my father in law," wrote Joseph, "and told him falsehoods concerning me, of the most shameful nature, which turned the old gentleman and his family so much against us, that they would no longer promise us protection, nor believe our doctrines."[38] With others in the

Harmony area turning against them as well, Joseph and Emma accepted the Whitmers' invitation to move to Fayette in the latter part of August. Emma would never see her parents again.

Joseph had been back to the Whitmer home in June to preside over the first general conference of the Church there, returning soon afterwards to Harmony. When he and Emma arrived at the Whitmer home in late August, arrangements were being made to hold the second general conference there. The anticipation was marred somewhat, however, when Joseph learned that Hiram Page, a son-in-law of the Whitmers and one of the Eight Witnesses of the Book of Mormon, had received two "revelations" through a stone, the contents of which, recorded Joseph, "were entirely at variance with the order of Gods house, as laid down in the new Testament, as well as in our late revelations."[39] Making matters worse, many Church members in the area—especially the Whitmers and Oliver Cowdery—accepted Page's revelations as legitimate. The crisis was solved after Joseph received what became section 28 in the Doctrine and Covenants, which teaches that members of the Church can receive revelation for themselves and as they "speak or teach" in the Church (D&C 28:4), but only one person—the prophet—can receive revelation for the Church at large.

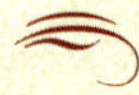

Joseph received several additional revelations in the Whitmer home during the days surrounding this second conference of the Church. Some provided instructions for individuals, while others, such as Doctrine and Covenants 29, addressed such topics as the last days, the Second Coming, and the fall of Adam. Important revelations, at least from a historical viewpoint, were those that called Peter Whitmer Jr. (D&C 30) and Parley P. Pratt and Ziba Peterson (D&C 32) to accompany Oliver Cowdery on a mission to the Lamanites. En route to the Indian Territory west of Missouri, the four men stopped for a time in northeastern Ohio to preach to friends and acquaintances of Parley P. Pratt. Their efforts resulted in the baptism of more than 120 people, including such notables as Frederick G. Williams, Sidney Rigdon, Algernon Sidney Gilbert, and John Murdock. Rigdon and another man, Edward Partridge, who believed the message but wanted to meet Joseph before being baptized, joined converts from other areas, including Orson Pratt and Thomas B. Marsh, in visiting Joseph at the Whitmer home during the last half of 1830.

Joseph's time in New York, which began in Palmyra the winter of 1816–17, ended in Fayette in January 1831. In connection with the third general conference of the Church—held, like the first two, in the Whitmer home—Joseph received two revelations (D&C 37 and 38) instructing him and the other Saints living in New York to move to Ohio. Settling his affairs the best he could and accompanied by Rigdon and Partridge, Joseph and Emma (who was pregnant with twins) left for Kirtland, Ohio, where they arrived in early February.

It had been almost eleven years since the First Vision in the Sacred Grove, during which time various sites in New York and Pennsylvania had served as the background for important events related to the restoration of the gospel in the latter days. Many of these places had changed little by the time Anderson arrived with his camera in 1907, allowing him to memorialize them for future generations of Latter-day Saints.

4

Ohio

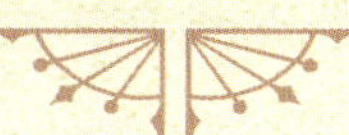

In 1907, George Edward Anderson made his way to a small village in northeastern Ohio to photograph sites associated with the Latter-day Saints when they "called Kirtland home."[1] There he captured several memorable images of the temple, a remarkable structure that had been built at great sacrifice by the early Saints and completed in 1836. Additionally, he took time to walk the dusty lanes of Kirtland, identifying and photographing homes built by the Saints when they gathered on the banks of the Chagrin River to build a thriving community there between 1831 and 1838.

> Gathering was one of the unique features of nineteenth-century Mormonism.

The gathering was one of the unique features of nineteenth-century Mormonism. Newly baptized members of the Church were asked by their leaders to move to specific geographical locations, a practice that ended in the late 1890s. Joining one of the popular Protestant churches, such as the Methodists, Baptists, or Presbyterians, did not require a convert to relocate. But accepting the message of the Restoration required the Saints to sell lands and homes, pack some belongings, and bid family and friends good-bye.

The people who joined the Church at this time took the first step on their individual and collective religious journeys the very moment they stepped through the threshold of their family home for the last time. Thus these first converts began a truly remarkable personal commitment that eventually took many of them to the western part of North America, where they established hundreds of communities extending from southern Alberta, Canada, to Mexico.

This extraordinary effort to build communities of faith and peace began with the call in December 1830 to "go to the Ohio" (D&C 37:1). This call came just eight months after the Church of Jesus Christ was organized on April 6, 1830. By this time, there were three small branches of the Church (Fayette, Colesville, and Manchester/Palmyra). In this important revelation, the Lord told the disciples that one of the reasons he commanded them to leave New York was because of "the enemy" (D&C 37:1). A few weeks later he further emphasized that going to Ohio would allow them to "escape the power of the enemy" (D&C 38:31).

Antagonism, violence, and extreme prejudice plagued Joseph Smith and the Saints in western New York. The Prophet first experienced opposition in the wake of the First Vision in 1820 (Joseph Smith–History 1:21–22). Harassment, which continued as the Restoration unfolded during the next few years, did not end with the organization of the Church in 1830. In fact, Joseph Smith and the Saints experienced intense persecution at Harmony and Colesville in the months after that singular event in Fayette, New York. As winter snows fell upon the New York landscape, the future looked bleak for members of the Church.

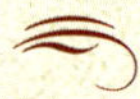

During the first half of the nineteenth century, America had not really begun the process of becoming a nation that not only tolerated religious, political, and social differences but also encouraged pluralism—the freedom to participate fully in the American experience even if a person or group did not agree with the majority's political, social, and religious opinions. Joseph Smith and the Saints were out of step with the majority and, as a result, experienced the full brunt of discrimination. The Prophet's enemies in New York used every possible means, including boycotts, physical violence, and legal prosecution in their efforts to stop the spread of the good news of the Restoration. It was in this setting that the Lord told the Saints to "go to the Ohio" (D&C 37:1).

In a revelation that followed, the Lord informed the Saints that he would gather "unto [himself] a righteous people, without spot and blameless" (D&C 38:31). The gathering, therefore, was a primary means of building a community of faith where people who truly repented of their sins could participate in sacred ordinances symbolizing the purity required to be found spotless and blameless before the Lord. Joseph Smith's mission was to build those communities, and the Saints' mission was to gather to them.

Although the move to Ohio presented challenges to the new Church, it also provided many opportunities.

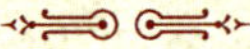

In this January 1831 revelation, the Lord continued, "Wherefore, for this cause [to gather a righteous people] I gave unto you the commandment that ye should go to the Ohio" (D&C 38:32). The Lord also promised the Saints two specific blessings if they responded to his call to gather "to the Ohio." First, he would give them his law (recorded today in D&C 42), and second, he would endow them with "power from on high" (D&C 38:32).

Strong echoes of the Exodus reverberate throughout the story, reminding us that the children of Israel fled Egypt (the land of their enemies) into the wilderness of Sinai, where they received blessings from the Lord, including his law (Exodus 19–20). There were no mountains in northeastern Ohio, but the Saints erected a temple where Jehovah revealed himself, as he had at Mount Sinai (D&C 110).[2]

Converts flocked to Ohio in fulfillment of the command to gather where Joseph Smith had established the Church headquarters in Kirtland, about twenty-five miles northeast of Cleveland, Ohio. What had once been a rather sleepy rural hamlet became an important economic, political, social, and religious center. When Anderson visited there in 1907, it had returned, by and large, to the quiet village it had been in February 1831 when Joseph Smith arrived there by sleigh from New York State. Only the temple, several marked graves in the cemetery, and a few houses built by the Saints revealed that this community had once been a gathering place of the Church.

Although the move to Ohio presented challenges to the new Church, it also provided many opportunities. For example, the Prophet had been inspired by the stories found in the Book of Mormon and the translation of Genesis (which he had begun

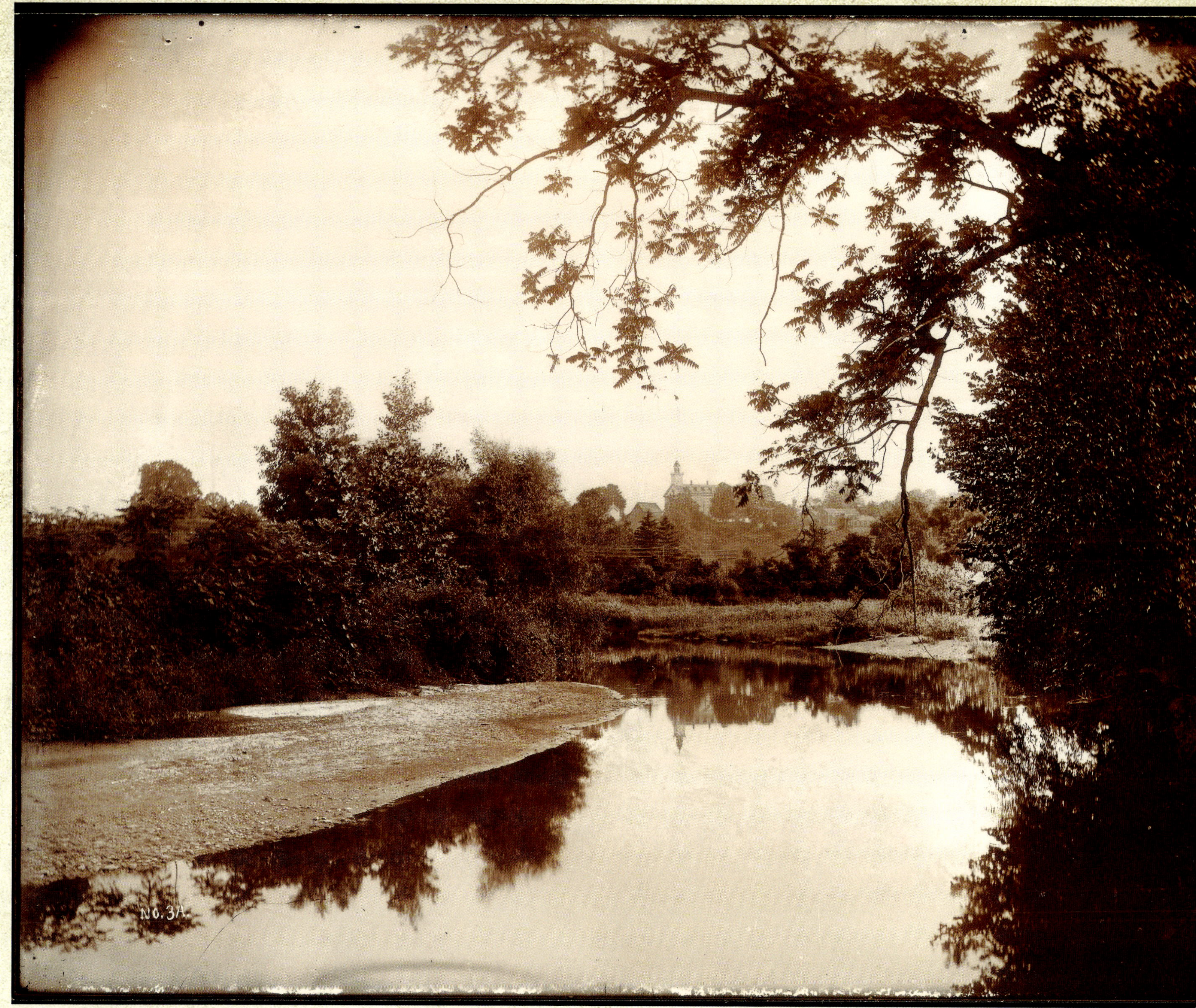

The Kirtland Temple, Kirtland, Ohio, August 7, 1907, Anderson Collection, LDS Church History Library, Salt Lake City, Utah.

in June 1830) about Enoch, the New Jerusalem, and Zion—a City of Holiness (Moses 7:19). In Ohio the Prophet was able to establish a city of faith based on revelations from God and, as he had been commanded for the first time, build and dedicate a temple to the Lord. Though establishing priesthood quorums and ordinances occupied much of the Prophet's time, the themes of city and temple building dominated his prophetic vision throughout his life.[3] Church leaders took this same vision of priesthood, temple, and city building to the Great Basin in 1847 to continue the work that the Prophet Joseph Smith had begun in Ohio.

Joseph Smith received thirty-eight revelations during his first year in Ohio. That number represents more than 28 percent of his canonized revelations found in the Doctrine and Covenants.[4] This remarkable period of revelation highlights the significance of Ohio not only for Joseph Smith and the early Saints but also for all those who are inspired by the same vision he shared with the Saints in the 1830s. The Ohio revelations, including those received in 1831, deal with timely and timeless principles. They give direction to the Church and to individuals on how to act and what to do. They reveal how the Lord unfolded his will to the early Saints on a variety of topics, from the Second Coming to the establishment of a house of God. Interestingly, a September 1831 revelation indicated that Kirtland would be "a strong hold" for only a few years (D&C 64:21); in fact, it was only a temporary place of refuge for the Saints.

Though establishing priesthood quorums and ordinances occupied much of the Prophet's time, the themes of city and temple building dominated his prophetic vision throughout his life.

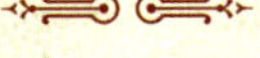

One important topic addressed by the 1831 revelations was the publication of Joseph Smith's revelations in book form. Beginning in 1828 and continuing throughout his life, the Prophet received revelation upon revelation, many of which he recorded. By November 1831 he had prepared, with the help of John Whitmer, a manuscript book identified as the "Book of Commandments and Revelations."[5] This manuscript book was apparently referred to in one of the November 1831 revelations: "Now, seek ye out of the *Book of Commandments,* even the least that is among them, and appoint him that is the most wise among you; or, if there be any among you that shall make one like unto it, then ye are justified in saying that ye do not know that they are true" (D&C 67:6–7; emphasis added).

When those present at a November 1831 conference of elders in Hiram, Ohio, decided to move forward with the publication of Joseph Smith's revelations, the Lord provided a stamp of approval when he gave to the Church and to the world the "preface unto the book of my commandments" and revelations (D&C 1:6).

The manuscript book was sent to Independence, Missouri, for publication. W. W. Phelps, the Church printer, published a few revelations from the collection serially in the Church's newspaper, *The Evening and the Morning Star.* Nevertheless, Phelps was engaged in printing the complete collection in 1833 in a book titled *A Book of Commandments, for the Government of the Church of Christ, Organized According to Law, on the 6th of April, 1830.* This effort to publish the revelations in book form ended when a mob attacked the printing office in July, destroying the press, most of the pages already printed, and Phelps's home, which served as the Church's printing office in Jackson County. Two more years elapsed before the revelations were finally published and released to the public. This time they were included in a two-part work titled *Doctrine and Covenants of the Church of the Latter Day Saints: Carefully Selected from the Revelations of God,* released in Kirtland, Ohio, in 1835.

A few months after the important November 1831 Church conference in Hiram, Ohio, where Church leaders decided to publish the revelations received by the Prophet, another important revelation came from the Lord. While Joseph

Smith and Sidney Rigdon were continuing their work on the translation of the Bible, they came to John 5:29 and were inspired to make a subtle change. While they "meditated upon these things, the Lord touched the eyes of [their] understanding and they were opened, and the glory of the Lord shone round about. And [they] beheld the glory of the Son, on the right hand of the Father" (D&C 76:19–20).[6]

Known today simply as "the Vision," this revelation proved to be an important watershed event in the Restoration. The Book of Mormon focuses on salvation and eternal life; this vision moved the focus from individual salvation and the gift of eternal life to exaltation and eternal lives in families. Historian Richard Lyman Bushman observed: "A long February [1832] revelation, called 'The Vision,' returned to the question of human destiny. . . . It was the first of four revelations [D&C 76; 84; 88; 93] over the next fifteen months introducing the theme of exaltation. To the fundamentals of sin and atonement, the exaltation revelations added visions of life after salvation." He continued: "Salvation through Christ appeared on page after page of the *Book of Mormon* and again in the summary of beliefs prepared at the organization of the Church. 'The Vision' went on from there, dwelling less on reconciliation with God than on achieving the highest realms of God's glory."[7]

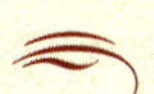

In addition to these doctrines, the Lord revealed his economic law, known today as the law of consecration. The first mention of it was in February 1831: "And behold, thou wilt remember the poor, and consecrate of thy properties for their support that which thou hast to impart unto them, with a covenant and a deed which cannot be broken. And inasmuch as ye impart of your substance unto the poor, ye will do it unto me; and they shall be laid before the bishop of my church" (D&C 42:30–32).

This law was revealed over time, and aspects of it are found scattered throughout the revelations of the Ohio period. These revelations revealed not only the eternal purposes and principles that governed this law but also immediate instructions on how to implement it during this period of Church history. Additionally, the Lord expanded the priesthood organization to meet the needs of a growing Church by establishing new priesthood offices, including bishops, high priests, patriarchs, and seventies. Eventually, the First Presidency, originally known as the Presidency of the High Priesthood, stake presidencies and high councils, the Quorum of the Twelve Apostles, and the quorum of seventy were organized in Kirtland and filled with men ordained to the priesthood.[8] This expansion of priesthood ordinations had a remarkable effect upon the Church. Richard Bushman asserted, "In a democratic time, the Mormons emerged as the most democratic of the churches, rivaled only by the Quakers."[9]

The Lord revealed his economic law, known today as the law of consecration, and expanded the priesthood organization.

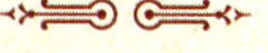

The main duty of all those ordained to the priesthood was to preach the gospel of Jesus Christ. The Prophet sent missionaries across the United States, Canada, and eventually to the British Isles to seek converts as the work expanded. This missionary activity meant that at any given time a large number of men were away from their families on missionary journeys. The women of the Church knew from experience what a call to the priesthood entailed—a mission assignment. Caroline Crosby related her own experience:

"Shortly after our arrival [in Kirtland], my husband

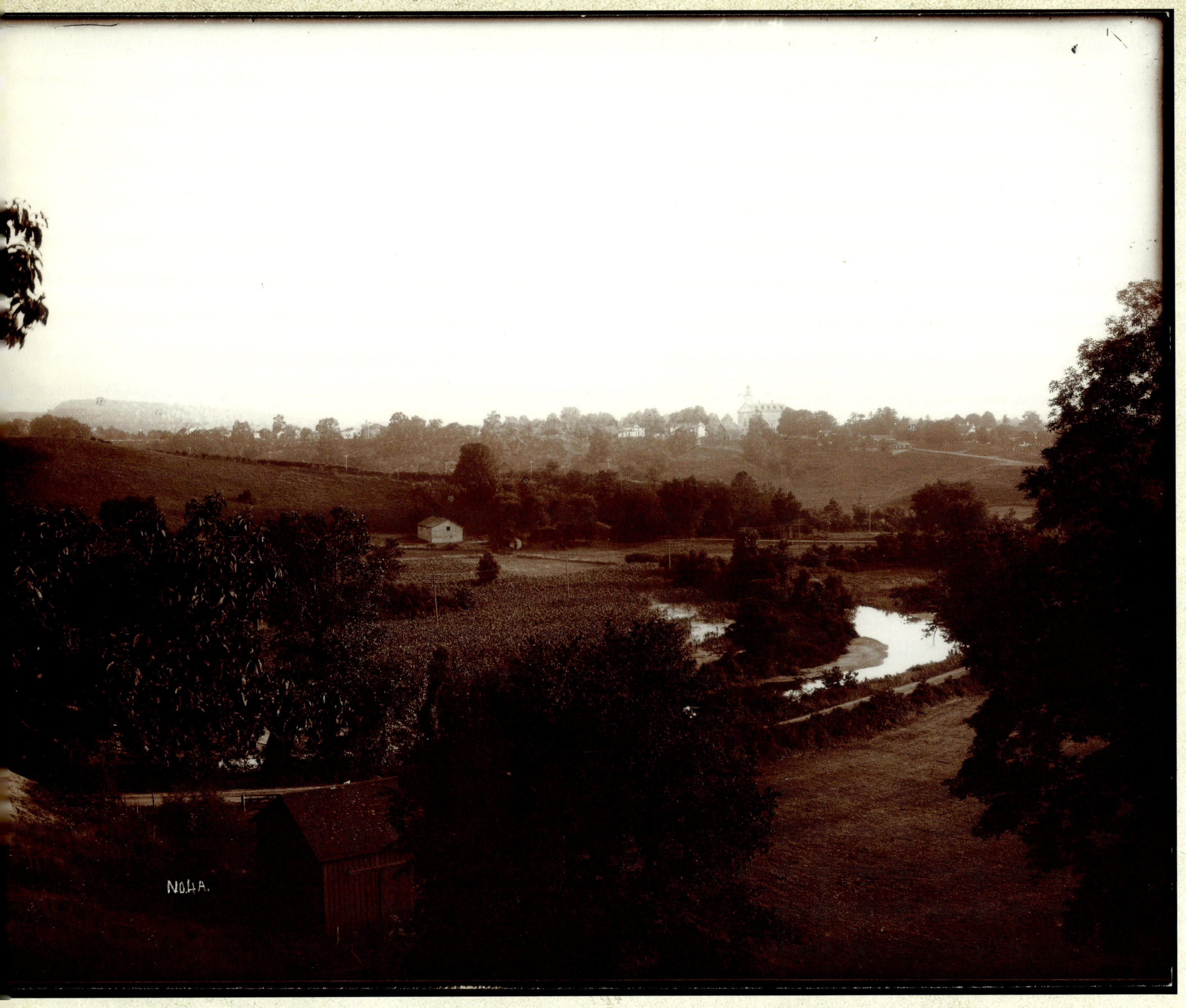

View of the Kirtland Temple on the bluff, Kirtland, Ohio, August 6 or 7, 1907, Anderson Collection, LDS Church History Library, Salt Lake City, Utah.

was ordained to the office of an elder. . . . I well recollect the sensation with which my mind was actuated when I learned the fact that my husband had been called and ordained to the Melchizedek priesthood and would undoubtedly be required to travel and preach the gospel to the nations of the earth."[10]

Church leaders, including Joseph Smith, were among the missionaries who left families and homes to preach the message of the Restoration. The expanding missionary effort increased the number of people gathering to Ohio in the 1830s.

The Prophet's efforts to translate the Bible, as he had

been commanded, had been interrupted by the call to gather to Ohio. Once he arrived there, however, he continued the work, and in July 1833 he finished the translation. Not only had he gone through the Old and New Testaments, but he also had inquired about the Apocrypha, a section of the Bible containing writing primarily created during the approximately four-hundred-year intertestamental period (from Malachi to John the Baptist). At the time most Protestant Bibles contained these three sections: the Old Testament, the Apocrypha, and the New Testament. The Prophet's work of translation produced many manuscript pages (the basis of the Joseph Smith Translation). In addition, several revelations came as a result of his work on the Bible (for example, D&C 76).

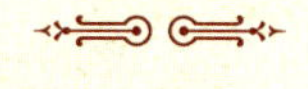

Joseph Smith prayed, thought, cried, dreamt, sang, and talked about Zion.

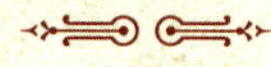

Joseph Smith prayed, thought, cried, dreamt, sang, and talked about Zion. From the time the Church was established in 1830, the Prophet and the Saints had been anxious to identify Zion's location. Joseph left Ohio in 1831 and traveled to western Missouri, where the Lord identified the spot for the temple that would be the focus of the city of Zion in the last days (D&C 57:1–3). Soon Latter-day Saints began to gather to Jackson County, where they hoped to build the New Jerusalem. Turmoil erupted in Missouri, however, and the Saints were brutally driven from their homes, farms, and businesses in 1833. Most fled across the Missouri River to Clay County while others found refuge in adjoining counties during the winter of 1833 and 1834. Again the Prophet wept for Zion, wondering if and when she might be redeemed.

Beginning in February 1834, Joseph Smith responded to a revelation about the redemption of Zion (D&C 103:20–40) by enlisting volunteers to travel to Missouri to help the Saints return to their homes. By May 1834, Zion's Camp, as this group of men became known, was on the move with the Prophet at their head. Surprisingly, the Lord disbanded Zion's Camp just as it approached Jackson County (D&C 105:9). This was a challenging time for Joseph. Some participants were disappointed and upset that they were unable to redeem Zion. Additionally, some were also critical of the Prophet's leadership.

Upon his return from Missouri to Kirtland, Joseph Smith organized the Quorum of the Twelve Apostles, mostly veterans of Zion's Camp who shared the challenges, struggles, and dangers of the march to Missouri. The first were ordained on February 14, 1835. One month following the quorum's organization, the Lord told the Saints that the Twelve were "equal in authority and power" to the First Presidency, which nevertheless still presided over them (D&C 107:23–24; see also 112:20, 30). An important doctrinal piece of the foundation for succession in the presidency of the Church was now in place. Further developments would occur in Nauvoo that made this even clearer.

Begun in June 1833, the construction of the house of the Lord, a multiuse building in Kirtland, remained in 1835 and 1836 one of the chief concerns of the Saints. It has often been observed that the Prophet did not construct any traditional meetinghouses during his ministry but instead focused all of his building activities on temples.

The command to build a temple in Kirtland was given in a meeting with the high priests in December 1832 when Joseph Smith received a revelation known today as the "Olive Leaf" (D&C 88). In it the Lord commanded the Saints to "sanctify yourselves that your minds become single to God, and the days will come that you shall see him" (D&C 88:68). Joseph learned that this "great and last promise" could be accomplished only after they had washed their hands and feet and come together united in a solemn assembly (D&C 88:74). Shortly after the revelation was received, the Prophet wrote Church leaders in Missouri: "You will see that the Lord commanded us in Kirtland to build an house of God, & establish a school for the Prophets, this is the word of the Lord to us, & we must yea the Lord helping us we will obey, as on conditions of our obedience, he has promised <us> great things, yea <even> a visit from the heavens to honor us with his own presence."[11]

Beginning in the summer of 1833, the Prophet spent the next three years building the house of the Lord and preparing the Saints to receive the promised blessings in the Kirtland Temple once it was completed. He did this primarily through meetings held in various locations throughout Kirtland in a variety of settings (school, quorum, and public meetings). In November 1835, for example, he met with the Twelve Apostles and challenged them:

"We must have all things prepared and call our solemn assembly as the Lord has commanded us [D&C 88:70], that we may be able to accomplish his great work: and it must be done in God's own way, the house of the Lord must be prepared, and the solemn assembly called and organized in it according to the order of the house of God, and in it we must attend to the ordinance of washing of feet; it was never intended for any but official members; it is calculated to unite our hearts, that we may be one in feeling and sentiment and that our faith may be strong, so that Satan cannot overthrow us, nor have any power over us—the endowment you are so anxious about you cannot comprehend now, nor could Gabriel explain it to the understanding of your dark minds, but strive to be prepared in your hearts, be faithful in all things that when we meet in the solemn assembly that is such as God shall name out of all the official members, will meet, and we must be clean every whit."[12]

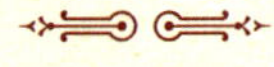

Beginning in the summer of 1833, the Prophet spent the next three years building the house of the Lord and preparing the Saints to receive the promised blessings in the Kirtland Temple.

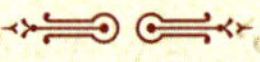

W. W. Phelps reflected: "Our meetings will grow more and more solemn, and will continue till the great solemn assembly when the house is finished! We are preparing to make ourselves clean, by first cleansing our hearts, forsaking our sins, forgiving every body; putting on clean decent clothes, by anointing our heads and by keeping all the commandments. As we come nearer to God we see our imperfections and nothingness plainer and plainer."[13]

By January 1836, priesthood leaders began meeting to perform the ordinances outlined in the Olive Leaf revelation in preparation for the solemn assembly to be held at the temple (D&C 88). Oliver Cowdery observed:

"And after pure water was prepared, called upon the Lord and proceeded to wash each other's bodies, and bathe the same with whiskey, perfumed with cinnamon. This we did that we might be clean before the Lord for the Sabbath, confessing our sins and covenanting to be faithful to God. While performing this washing with solemnity, our minds were filled with many reflections upon the propriety of the same, and how the priests anciently used to wash always before ministering before the Lord."[14] In a candlelit meeting on January 21, 1836, Church leaders gathered in the western room of the attic offices on the third floor of the nearly completed

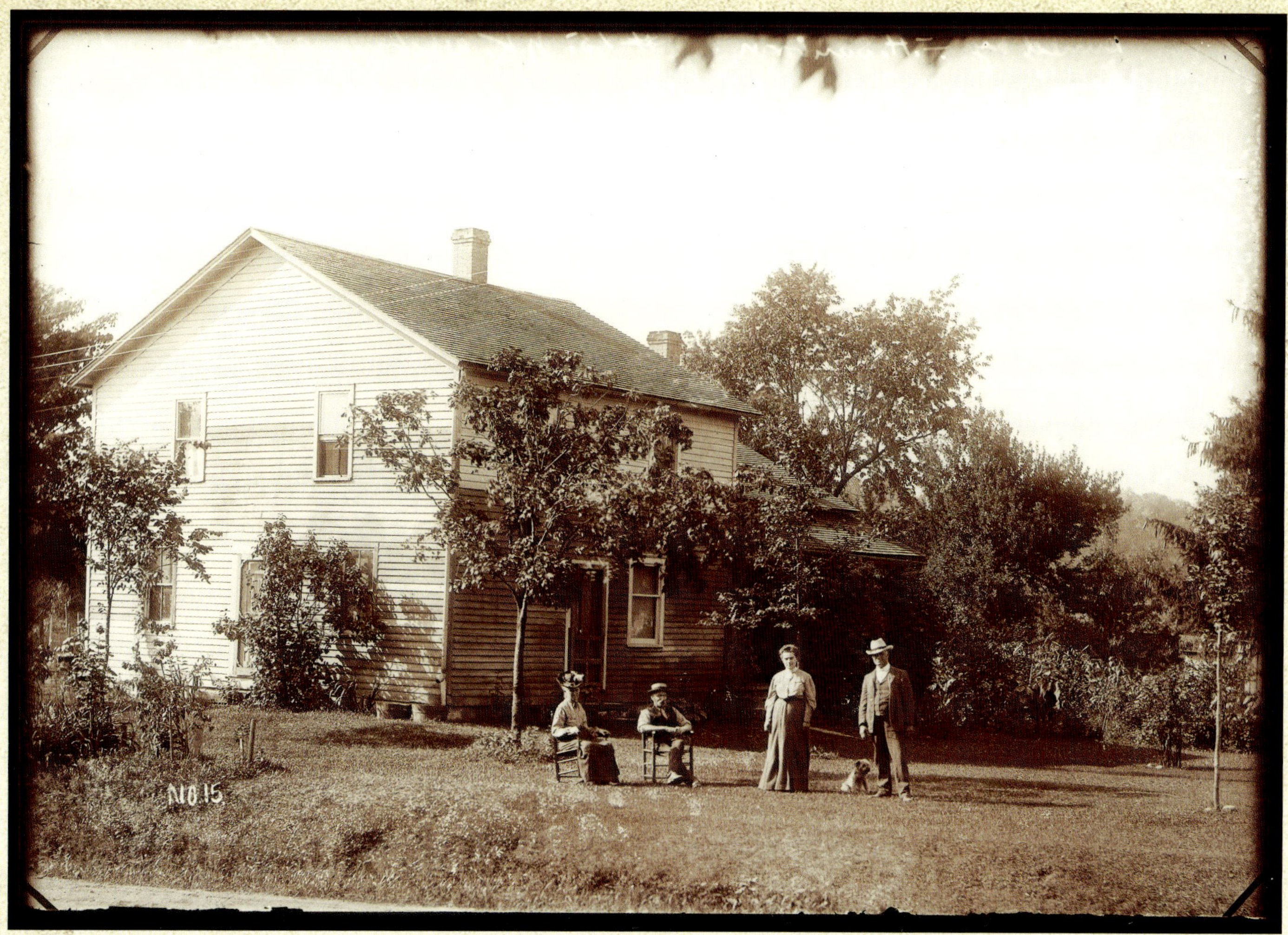

Home of Newel Kimball and Elizabeth Ann Smith Whitney, Kirtland, Ohio, August 7, 1907, Anderson Collection, LDS Church History Library, Salt Lake City, Utah.

house of the Lord to complete the ordinances performed earlier in the day in the loft of the printing office (washing their bodies with pure water and anointing their heads "in the name of the Lord").[15] On this occasion they consecrated oil, anointed each other, and pronounced blessings upon each other as inspired by the Lord.

During this gathering, Joseph Smith saw "the celestial kingdom of God" (D&C 137:1). Oliver Cowdery noted that "the glorious scene is too great to be described. . . . I only say, that the heavens were opened to many, and great and marvelous things were shown." Others also "saw visions & others were blessed with the outpouring of the Holy Ghost."[16]

When Joseph Smith recorded the vision he had witnessed in his journal, a record of an important revelation was preserved in detail, laying the foundation of salvation for the dead that would continue to be unfolded in Nauvoo.[17]

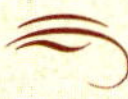

During the next few weeks and months, the Saints completed the temple and prepared to meet in a solemn assembly as directed in a December 1832 revelation (D&C 88:70, 117). In preparation for the first temple dedication in this dispensation, Joseph Smith and Oliver Cowdery wrote, through revelation, a rather lengthy prayer (D&C 109).[18] On the following day, March 26, 1836, the temple was opened, and within a short time it was filled with more than nine hundred Saints. Services began at nine o'clock and consisted of choir singing, scripture reading, prayers,

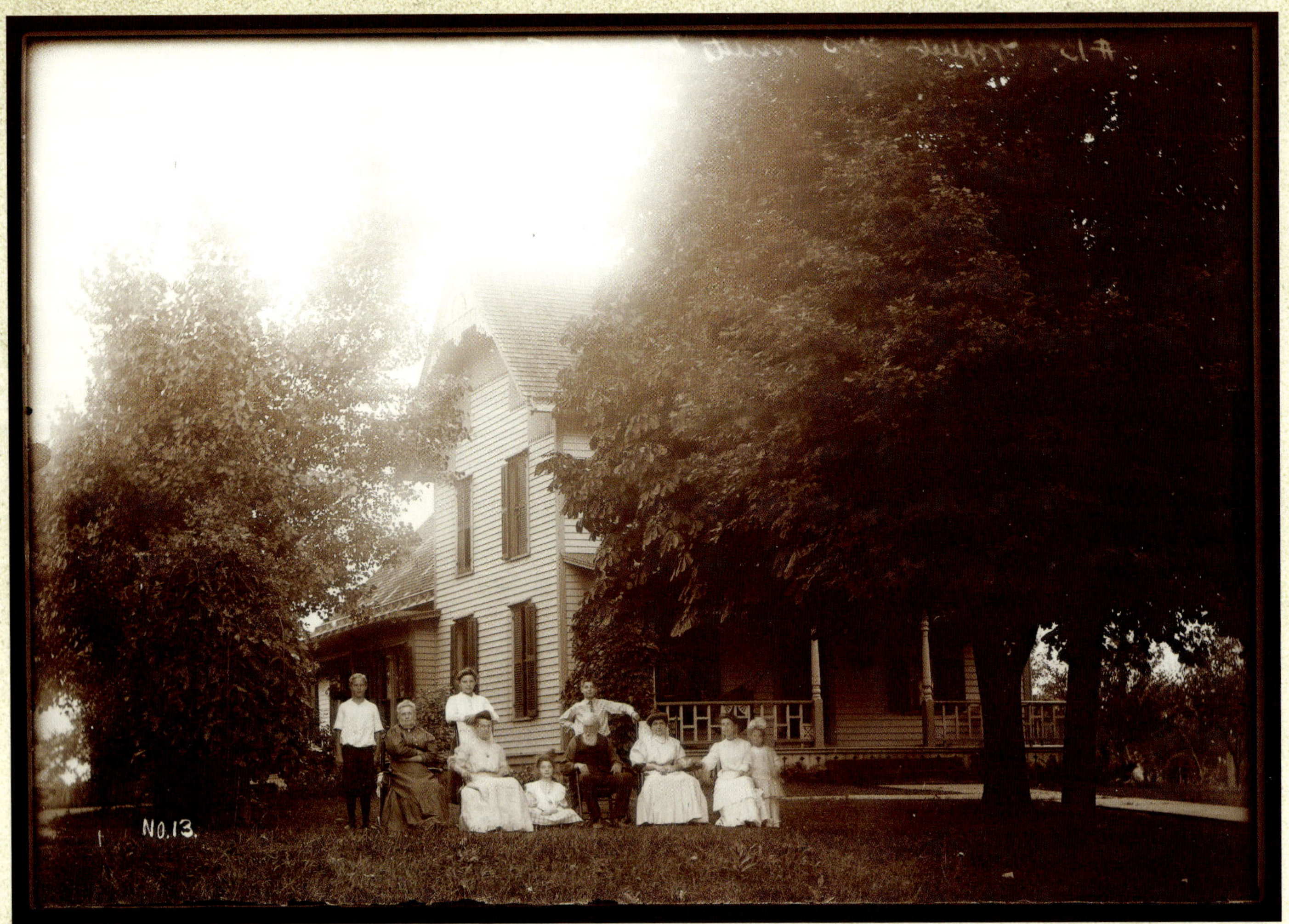

Home of Joseph and Emma Hale Smith, Kirtland, Ohio, August 7, 1907, Anderson Collection, LDS Church History Library, Salt Lake City, Utah.

Church business, and some lengthy sermons. Joseph Smith read the dedicatory prayer word for word—a tradition that continues in the Church today.

The dedicatory prayer echoed many of the themes found in Doctrine and Covenants 88, the Kirtland Temple revelation. Joseph Smith ended this prayer with the repetition "O hear, O hear, O hear us, Oh Lord!" (D&C 109:78) and then a final request that the Lord would enable the Saints gathered in the house of the Lord to "mingle [their] voices with those bright, shining seraphs around thy throne, with acclamations of praise, singing Hosanna to God and the Lamb! And let these, thine anointed ones, be clothed with salvation, and thy saints shout aloud for joy. Amen, and Amen" (D&C 109:79–80).

Joseph Smith read the dedicatory prayer word for word—a tradition that continues in the Church today.

The visions, heavenly voices, singing, and manifestation of the Holy Spirit continued to be poured out on the Saints. The Prophet wrote on March 30, 1836: "It was a Pentecost and enduement [endowment] indeed, long to be remembered, for the sound shall go forth from this place into all the world, and the occurrences of this day shall be handed down upon the pages of sacred history to all generations, as the day of Pentecost, so shall this day

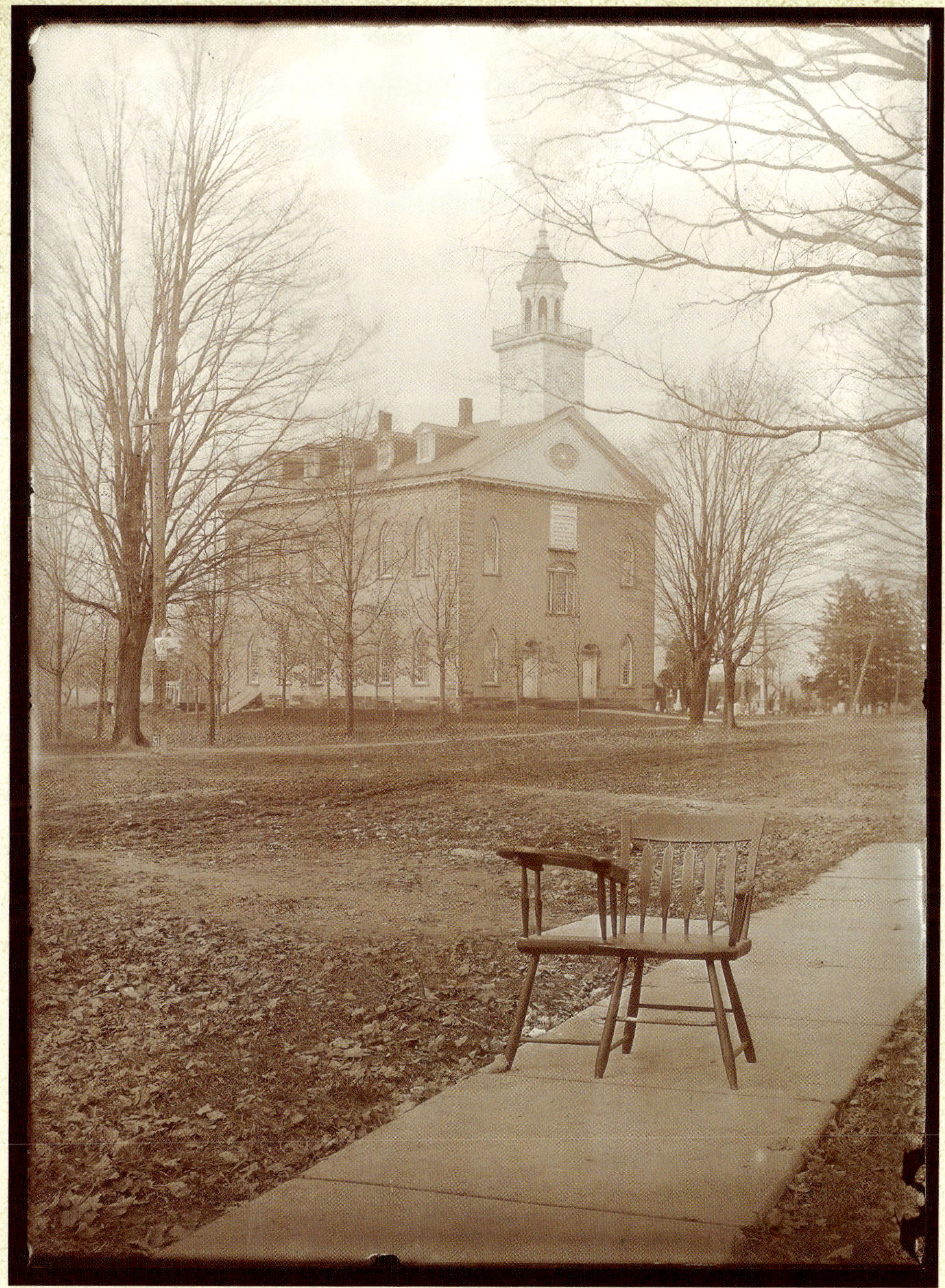

The Kirtland Temple, Kirtland, Ohio, August 7, 1907, Anderson Collection, LDS Church History Library, Salt Lake City, Utah.

be numbered and celebrated as a year of Jubilee and time of rejoicing to the saints of the most high God."[19]

On Easter Sunday, April 3, 1836, just a week following the temple dedication, Joseph Smith and Oliver Cowdery attended a meeting in the temple. After the administration of the sacrament, they retired to one of the pulpits (traditionally identified as the Melchizedek pulpits on the main floor of the temple), where the heavy curtains of the temple that allowed the Saints to divide the room into small meeting places were lowered. Here they bowed in a "solemn, but silent prayer to the Most High."[20] The heavens opened and the Lord stood before them, "standing upon the breastwork of the pulpit" (D&C 110:2). He spoke to them, forgiving them of their sins and pronouncing them clean before him.

Joseph Smith recorded, "After this vision closed, the heavens were again opened unto us; and Moses appeared before us, and committed unto us the keys of the gathering of Israel" (v. 11). "After this, Elias appeared, and committed the dispensation of the gospel of Abraham," which was followed by the appearance of Elijah (vv. 12–13). By the end of the revelation, additional keys of the dispensation of the fulness of times had been committed into the hands of Church leaders in preparation for further blessings that the Lord would give in Nauvoo.

Following the memorable dedication of the temple and the spiritual outpourings in 1836 came the Prophet's most challenging year to date. As historian Ronald K. Esplin has observed, the year 1837 "was emotionally disastrous and ended in apostasy and division."[21] Nevertheless, Joseph Smith remained resilient. "He believed in his calling. He believed in the revelations. And partly because of this faith, and maybe also because of the constitution and will he was born with, he could rise, time and again, from the ashes of defeat and do something even better."[22]

The 1837 Kirtland crisis is also known as the Kirtland apostasy. The apostasy was significant: It has been estimated that one-third of the Church's leadership lost its way at this time.

Many factors have been examined to explain the crisis. Scholars generally focus their attention on the nationwide economic downturn, known to economists and historians as the Panic of 1837, as the main cause of the Kirtland apostasy. The failure of many banks in the United States, including the Kirtland Safety Society Anti-Banking Company, were symptoms of a national depression in which property values plummeted, creating an economic crisis in many places, including Kirtland.

Disappointment and anger over the failure of the Kirtland Safety Society Anti-Banking Company caused some members of the Church to question Joseph Smith's prophetic claims (he had been involved in the establishment of the institution). Additionally, some members and nonmembers of the Church became embittered toward the Prophet when they saw their economic fortunes decline during the panic.

In the end, however, the battle for the hearts and souls in Kirtland is best understood as a cultural war within the Church. Esplin argues: "There was a cultural war going on in the Church in 1837 over what Joseph Smith was trying to introduce: a new way of thinking about society and religion based on ancient scripture models and modern revelation. This was the model of Enoch leading his people or Moses at the head of the children of Israel, where a religious leader had a great deal to say about everyday life and about how society was organized. This model was not the American way, nor is it today."[23]

He observes: "Some liked the American civil religion, as it has sometimes been called. They liked the idea that they were free as Americans to do their business six days a week and on the seventh day go to church where a preacher would teach them morals and maybe a little doctrine. But they did not expect this preacher to interject himself into their politics, their property, or their economic organization. This was the Protestant model, the model most early Latter-day Saints grew up with."[24]

The English converts traveled in droves to Nauvoo and later to Utah, carrying with them their testimony of the restored gospel, loyalty to the Twelve, and skills and financial resources that allowed the Church to achieve Joseph Smith's vision.

During this difficult period, Joseph Smith, acting upon divine inspiration, approached Heber C. Kimball during a meeting in the temple. The Prophet told Elder Kimball that he, as a member of the Twelve Apostles, would lead a mission to the British Isles for the salvation of the Church.[25] The Prophet said on that occasion, "God revealed to me that something new must be done for the salvation of His Church."[26] What Elder Kimball (and others who accompanied him) did in the British Isles was exactly that—they did indeed help to save the Church. Within one year, more than two thousand people had been baptized, and that was just the beginning of the great harvest of souls in England. These converts traveled in droves to Nauvoo and later to Utah, carrying with them their testimony of the restored gospel, loyalty to the Twelve, and skills and financial resources that allowed the Church to achieve Joseph Smith's vision.

The situation in Kirtland continued to deteriorate. Within a short time dissent, doubt, and desertion had severely weakened the Church in Ohio. Joseph and Sidney Rigdon received a revelation that confirmed that their labors were "finished in this place for a season" and instructed them to leave with their families for Missouri "as soon as it is practicable."[27]

Joseph Smith's escape from Kirtland on January 12, 1838, signaled the beginning of the end of the story of the Latter-day Saints in Ohio for a number of years. Eventually, the Prophet's family and other loyal Saints followed Joseph Smith to Missouri, nearly nine hundred miles away. Here the settlement of Far West, in Caldwell County, became the new headquarters of the Church of Jesus Christ.

5

Missouri

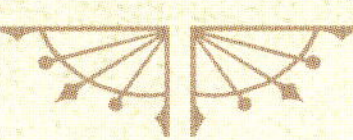

The sites George Edward Anderson photographed in Missouri embody some of the greatest hopes and bitterest disappointments of the early Church. Designated by the Lord as "the center place" for the city of Zion (D&C 57:2–3), Independence and the temple lot there were the focus of attention in the Church long after mobs drove the Saints from Jackson County in the fall of 1833. While waiting for Zion to be redeemed—that is, for the Saints to be able to return to Jackson County—Church members settled in and created dozens of other communities in the northern part of the state. Chief among these were Far West in Caldwell County and Adam-ondi-Ahman in Daviess County, the latter site identified through revelation as the "place where Adam shall come to visit his people" before the Second Coming of the Lord (D&C 116:1).

Missouri lawlessness and apostate jealousies had penetrated even into these relatively sparsely settled regions by the fall of 1838, however, resulting in the martyrdom of Elder David W. Patten after the battle of Crooked River, the massacre of seventeen Latter-day Saints at Haun's Mill, and the arrest of Joseph Smith at Far West. Stripped of their property and their leader, subjected to the abuse of mobs, and finding themselves the object of Governor Lilburn W. Boggs's extermination order, thousands of Saints fled the state in early 1839 as Joseph and other leaders awaited trial in the Liberty and Columbia jails on trumped-up charges. Anderson's well-composed photographs add a unique dimension to the rich documentary history that has survived from this era of Church history.

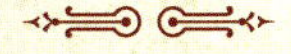

Jackson County entered Church history in 1831, when Oliver Cowdery and other missionaries took up residence there.

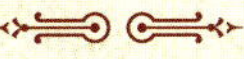

Jackson County entered Church history in 1831, when Oliver Cowdery and other missionaries took up residence there after officials refused them permission to preach in Indian Territory to the west. On June 7, 1831, Joseph learned that the city of Zion would be located somewhere in Missouri, with the precise location to be revealed after he and others—including the Colesville Branch (D&C 54)—traveled to the state (D&C 52:1–5). In mid-July, Joseph met with Oliver and the other missionaries in Independence—the principal town in Jackson County. On July 20 he learned through revelation that Independence was, in fact, the center place for the city of Zion, with "a spot for the temple . . . lying westward, upon a lot which is not far from

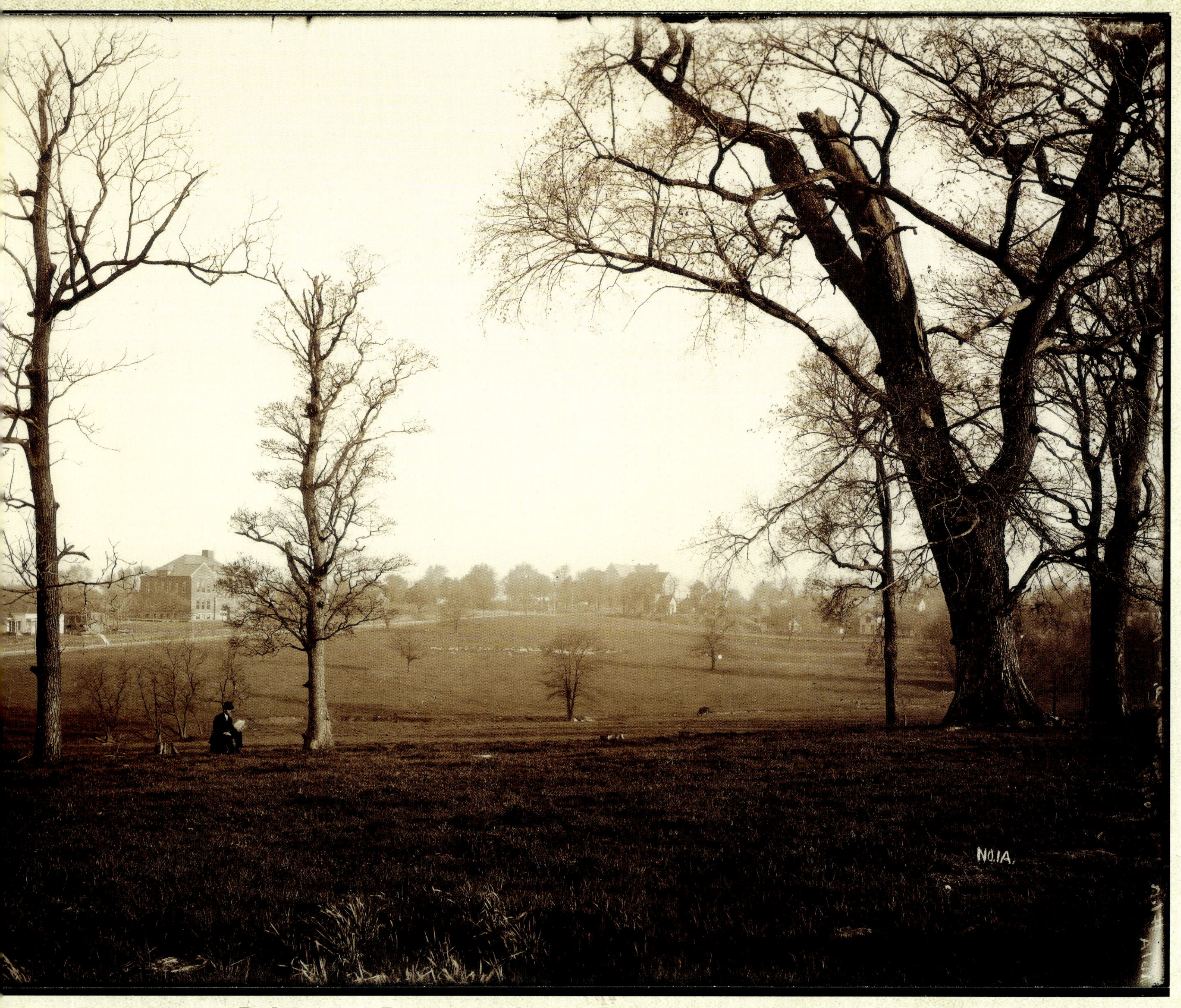

The Independence Temple property, Independence, Missouri, April 26, 1907, Anderson Collection, LDS Church History Library, Salt Lake City, Utah.

the courthouse" (D&C 57:3). On August 2, Sidney Rigdon dedicated the land of Zion for the gathering of the Saints, with Joseph dedicating the "spot for the Temple" the following day.[1] At the time, the ground was owned by Jones H. Flournoy; it did not come into Church hands until December 19, 1831, when Flournoy sold it to Edward Partridge for one hundred thirty dollars as part of a larger sixty-three-acre parcel.[2]

At the time of its dedication, the area was in "its wild state . . . covered with a heavy growth of timber," which Church members had "begun to remove for their present use" by March

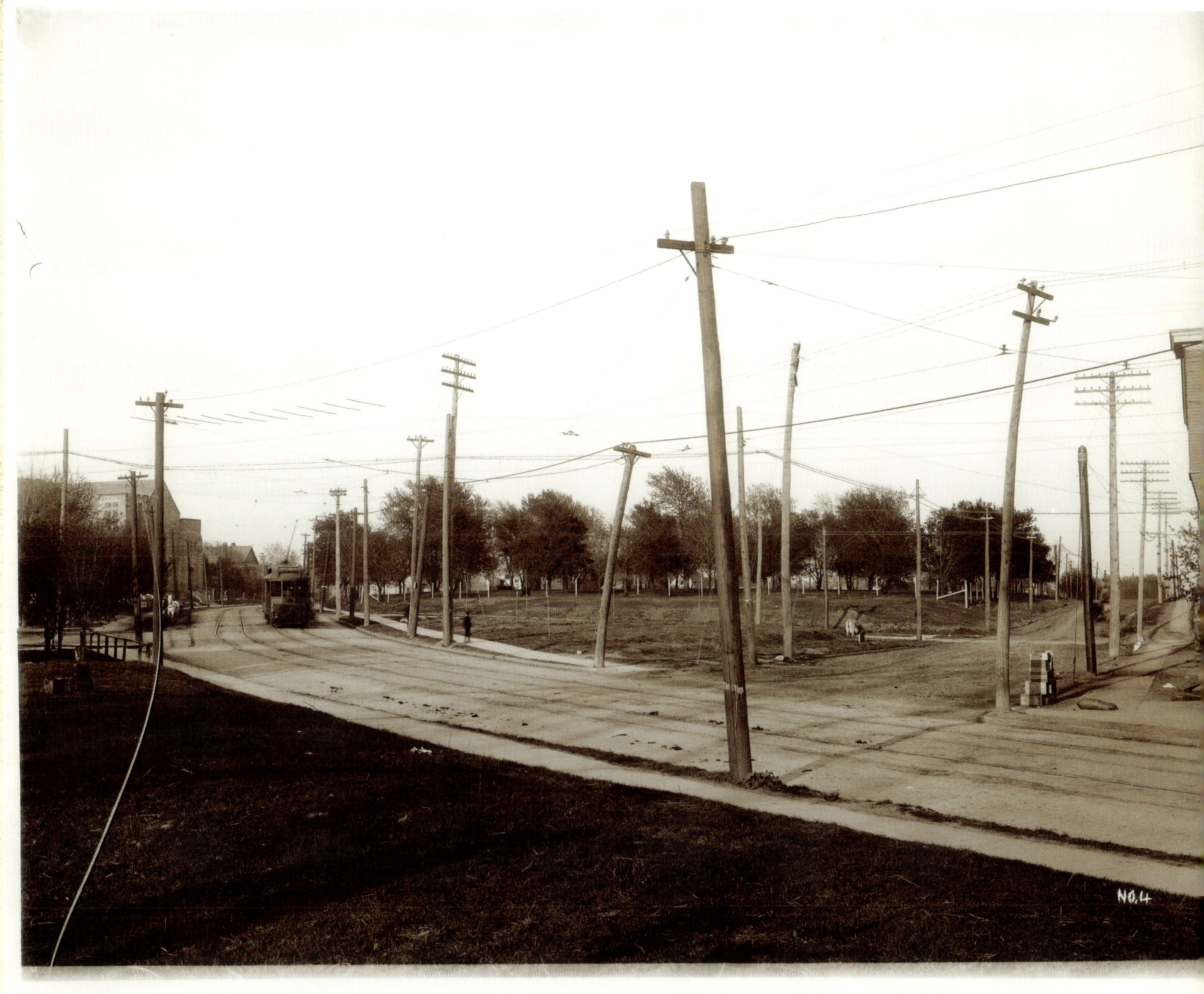

The temple lot, Independence, Missouri, April 26, 1907, Anderson Collection, LDS Church History Library, Salt Lake City, Utah.

1832.[3] As subsequent revelations would state, however, this plot of land was more than just a randomly chosen woodlot. The New Jerusalem itself, Joseph learned later, would be built "beginning at the temple lot," which had been "appointed by the finger of the Lord, in the western boundaries of the State of Missouri" (D&C 84:3). Development of the city, which would include construction on the temple lot, would literally begin "at this place, even the place of the temple" (D&C 84:4). Once built, the temple of the New Jerusalem would be filled with the "glory of the Lord" and serve as the repository for "an acceptable

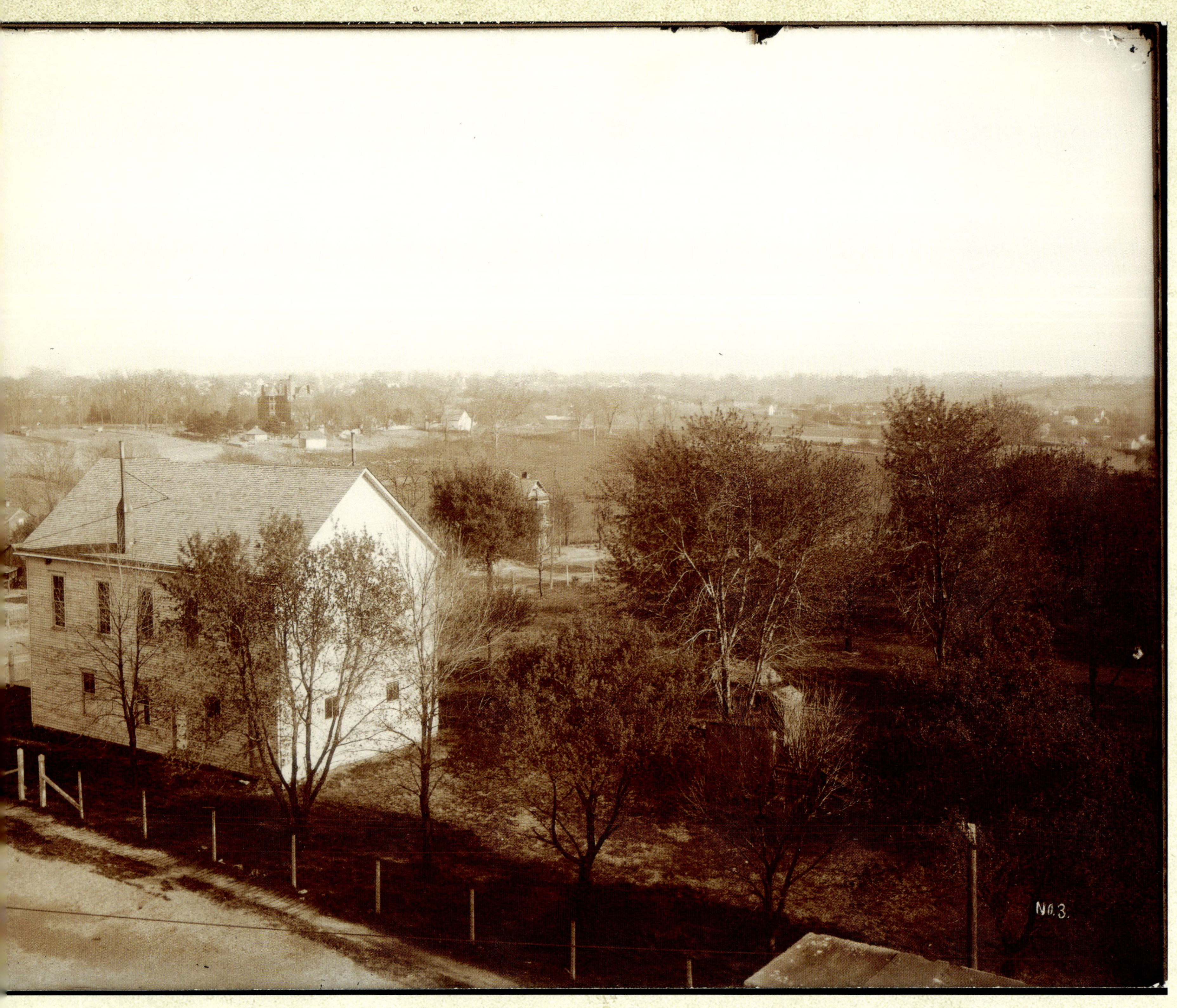

The Church of Christ (Temple Lot), Independence, Missouri, April 26, 1907, Anderson Collection, LDS Church History Library, Salt Lake City, Utah.

offering and sacrifice" to be offered by Church members in the latter days (D&C 84:5, 31; see also 128:24). The temple was, in short, to be the center of Zion and all that Zion is about—which probably explains Anderson's efforts to photograph the lot from a variety of angles and his choice of the area for the backdrop of a picture of Saints in the area.

Despite this understanding, it was not until June 1833, when Joseph drew up "the plat of the city of Zion," that the

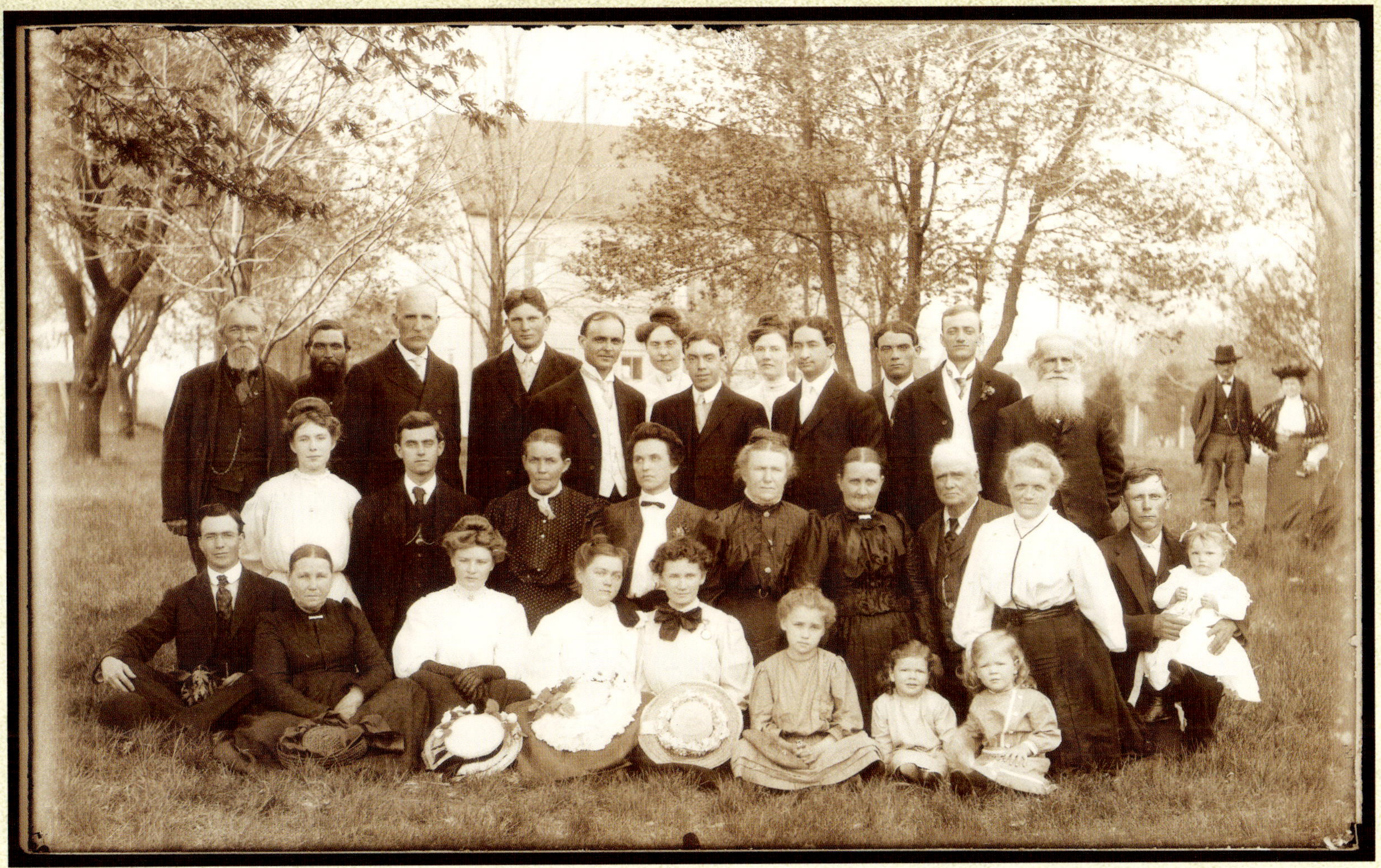

Latter-day Saints gathered on the temple lot, Independence, Missouri, April 28, 1907, Anderson Collection, LDS Church History Library, Salt Lake City, Utah.

Saints formally began to acknowledge the centrality of the temple lot in their building plans. As indicated on the plat, the original plan called for the "temple lot" to consist of two sixteen-acre blocks in the center of the city. Each block would contain twelve "temples," which Joseph variously defined as "public buildings, . . . houses of worship, schools, etc."[4] Those of the first block would be "for the use of the presidency"; those of the second, for the "lesser Priesthood."[5] Later plats drawn by Frederick G. Williams and Edward Partridge, which reduced each temple block to ten acres (matching the size of the city's residential blocks) and shifted the orientation of the blocks from a north-south axis to an east-west axis, indicate that plans for the temple lot were still fluid as late as August 1833.[6]

Notwithstanding the temple lot's cosmological significance, little had been done on it by the time the Saints were driven out of Jackson County in the fall of 1833. Several homes had been constructed on the lot—contrary to long-range plans—and at least two people, John and Rebecca Cordilia, who died during the expulsion were buried there, but work on the twenty-four temples per se was apparently limited to establishing, through a survey, the northeast and southeast corners of the northwestern-most temple to be built.[7] According to Joseph, this temple was to be one of three collectively called "House of the Lord, for the Presidency of the High and most Holy Priesthood, after the order of Melchizedek, which was after the order of the Son of God, upon Mount Zion, City of the New Jerusalem." Planned to be two stories high (with each story being fourteen feet high) and with outside dimensions of eighty-seven by sixty-one feet, this was to be the smallest of the twenty-four temples.[8]

The northeast and southeast corners of this temple were apparently marked with several survey stones found in 1929 during an excavation of the area by the Church of Christ (Temple Lot). An early offshoot of Mormonism, this church owns two and one-half acres of the temple lot today, including the area where the temple was to be built. Anderson's photograph of the church's white frame church gives a rough idea of where the temple was to be built and what the area looked like seventy years after the Saints were forced to abandon their property there.

The expulsion of the Saints from Jackson County in the fall of 1833 was the last of a series of violent acts against Church members there. Missourians had been harassing Saints since the spring of 1832, W. W. Phelps recorded, when "some persons, in the deadly hours of the night, commenced stoning or brick-batting some of our houses and breaking our windows."[9] These and similar minor, sporadic attacks escalated to organized mobocracy the following year when a well-planned, well-attended, and well-documented town meeting in Independence adjourned for two hours while a "committee of twelve" pressured Church leaders in the area to stop the Church's printing operations immediately and to "give a definite pledge of their intention, within a reasonable time to remove out of the county." Unsatisfied with the leaders' desire to consult "not only with their brethren here, but in Ohio" before making any such pledge, those attending the meeting then "resolved" to raze the Church's two-story printing building. According to the minutes of the meeting, the "resolution was forthwith carried into execution, as also some other steps of a similar tendency."[10]

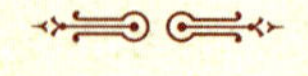

The expulsion of the Saints from Jackson County in the fall of 1833 was the last of a series of violent acts against Church members there.

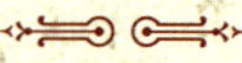

These "other steps" included tarring and feathering Edward Partridge and Charles Allen, destroying the Church's printing press, and threatening to destroy Algernon Sidney Gilbert's store. Church leaders signed an agreement to leave three days later to avert further violence but then quietly began looking for allies to help them stay on their lands. Learning of the Saints' intentions at the end of October, forty to fifty men attacked a branch of the Church in the western part of the county on the night of October 31. Subsequent attacks in and around Independence over the course of the next several days left the Saints with no alternative but to flee the county.

The Saints did, however, make at least one determined stand against the Missourians before leaving. This took place near the Mormon settlement on the Big Blue River, which crossed the main east-west road five miles west of Independence. Seven months earlier, on April 6, 1833, seventy to eighty members of the Church had met at the ferry there (run by Orrin Porter Rockwell and his father, Orin) and celebrated the third anniversary of the organization of the Church—the first time, reportedly, that the anniversary had been formally observed.[11]

On November 4, however, the area presented a very different picture. Rather than a group of celebrating Saints, a large party of Missourians met at the ferry, where they commandeered the ferryboat and threatened the lives of Church members in the area. Then they retired one mile west to a store, where word arrived of a small group of Mormon men nearby on their way to help members on the east side of the river. The

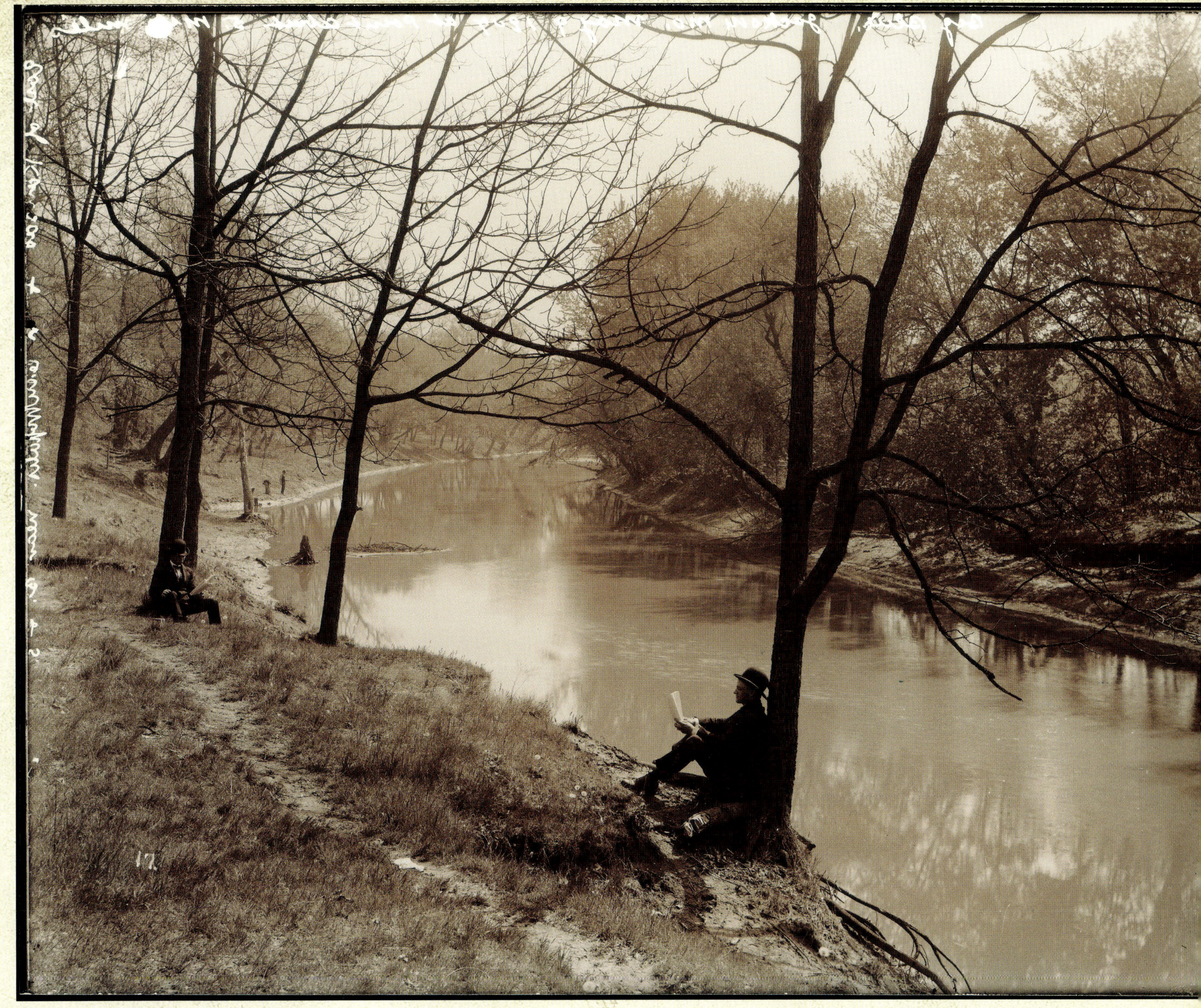

Mormon settlement site, 1831–33, on Big Blue River, Missouri, May 9, 1907, Anderson Collection, LDS Church History Library, Salt Lake City, Utah.

mob dispersed the small band of Mormons, only to be met by thirty others, led by David Whitmer, from farther west. In the ensuing gun battle—the Battle of the Blue, it has come to be called—two Missourians and one Latter-day Saint, Andrew Barber, were killed, while several on both sides were wounded. One of these, Philo Dibble, was miraculously healed after receiving a blessing from Newel Knight. In answer to the Saints' resistance at the Blue, Lt. Governor Lilburn W. Boggs called out

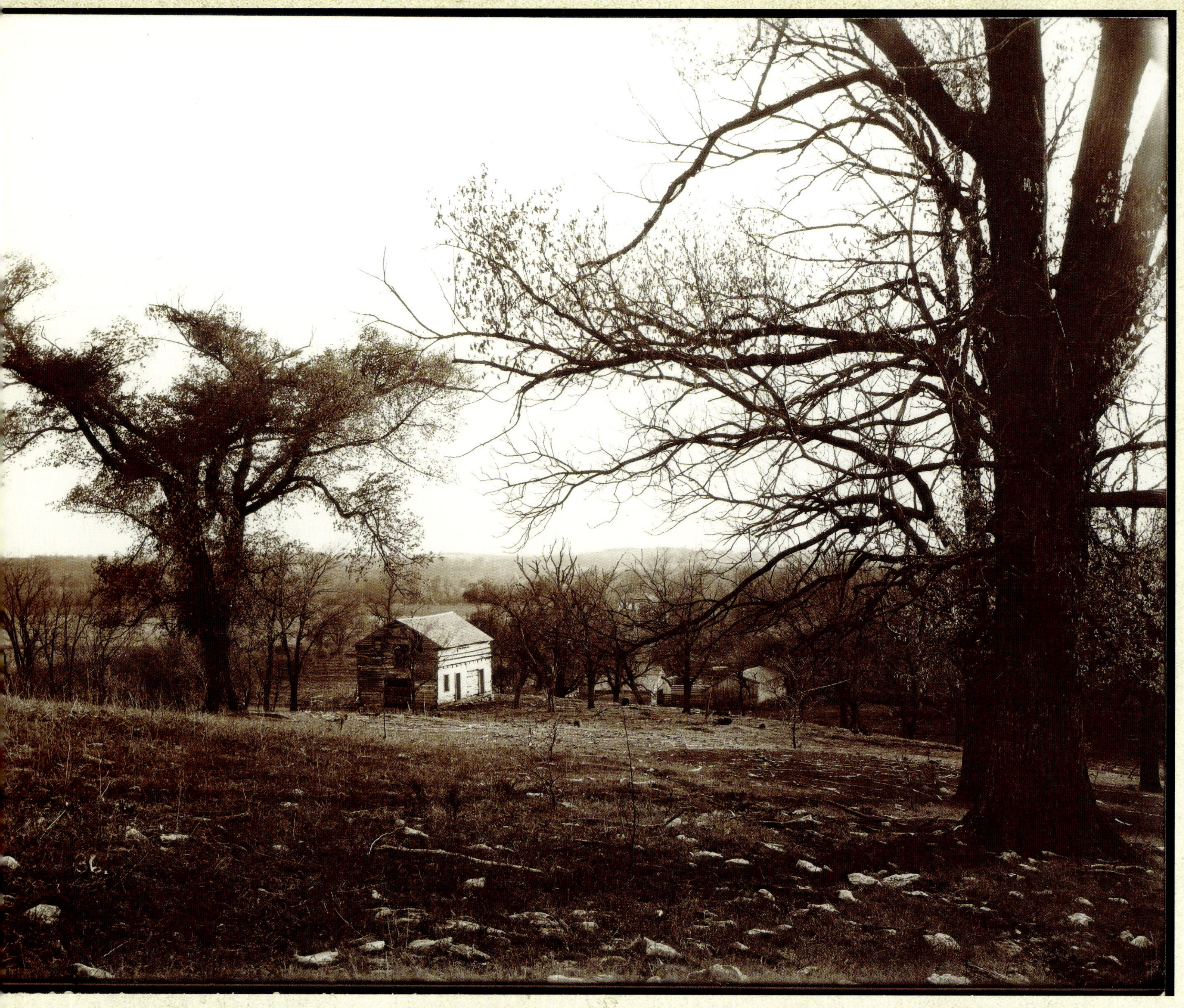

Second cabin of Lyman and Harriet Benton Wight, Adam-ondi-Ahman, Daviess County, Missouri, May 20, 1907, Anderson Collection, LDS Church History Library, Salt Lake City, Utah.

the militia the following day and ordered the Saints to surrender their guns, opening the way for mobs to drive them from the county without fear of reprisal.

With the expulsion from Jackson County, the Saints' fortunes shifted to northern Missouri. From the fall of 1833 to the summer of 1836, most lived in Clay County, where their numbers swelled to several thousand. From there the Church moved to unsettled land in central Ray County to the north and east, where they began building Far West and other settlements. Joseph and most of the Kirtland Saints joined them in 1838,

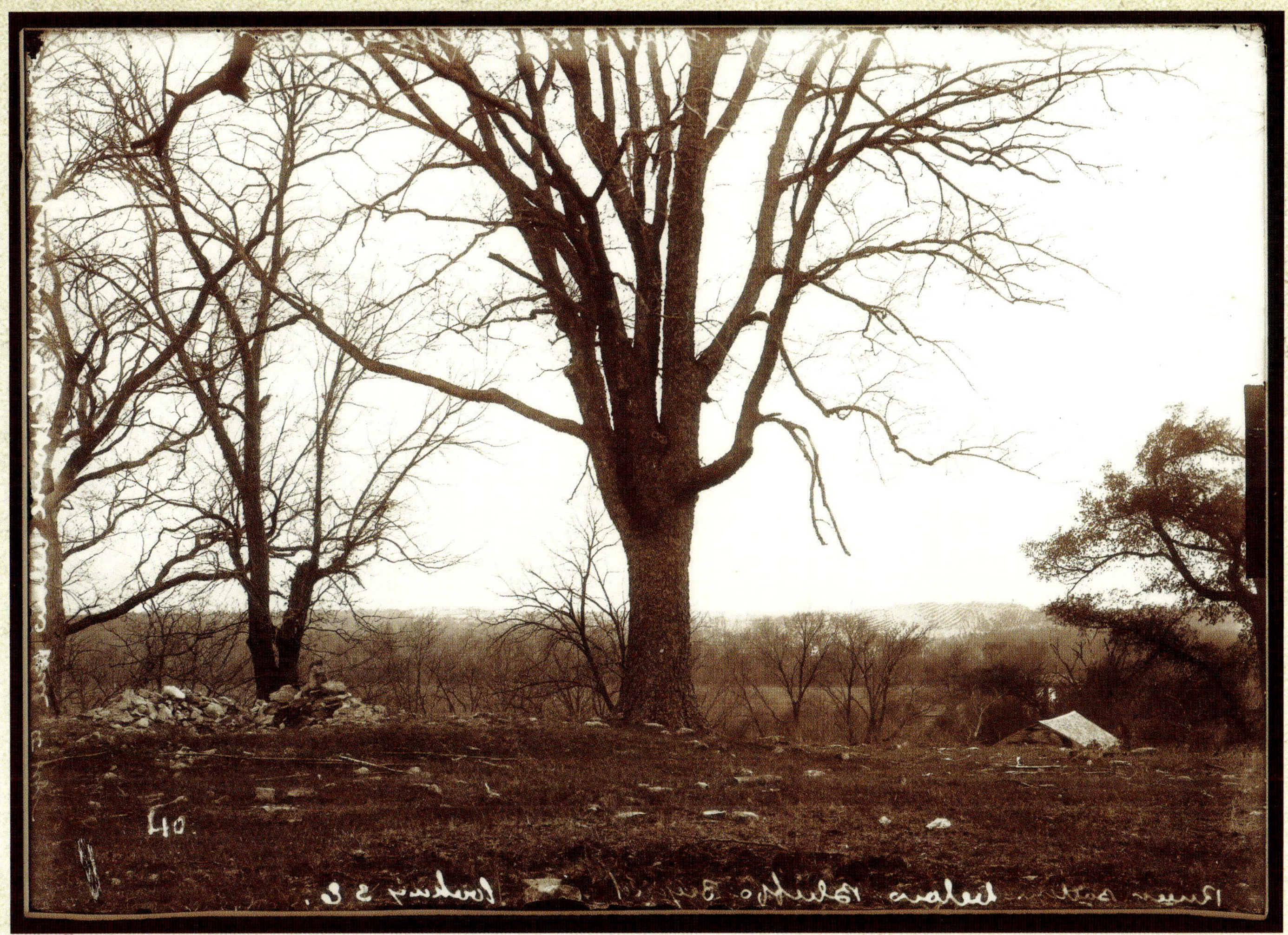

The Valley of Adam-ondi-Ahman from Tower Hill, Daviess County, Missouri, May 20, 1907, Anderson Collection, LDS Church History Library, Salt Lake City, Utah.

by which time the Missouri State Legislature had created two new counties out of Ray County's northern regions—Caldwell, where Far West was located and most of the Latter-day Saints lived; and Daviess to the north, where a few Missourians had settled.

Most Missourians assumed, or at least hoped, that the Latter-day Saints would confine their settlements in Missouri to Caldwell County, but such was not the case. Learning of the need for ferry service across the Grand River in Daviess County, Church member Lyman Wight and several others moved there in 1837 to a place they named Spring Hill. Joseph visited Wight and the other Saints at Spring Hill in May 1838, where he learned through revelation that the area was known to the Lord as Adam-ondi-Ahman—"the place where Adam shall come to visit his people, or the Ancient of Days shall sit, as spoken of by Daniel the Prophet" (D&C 116:1). Anderson's photographs of Diahman, as it came to be called, feature Lyman Wight's second cabin built on the side of Tower Hill—so named for "the remains of an old Nephitish Altar and Tower" on its summit[12]—and the view of the Grand River Valley, or Valley of Adam-ondi-Ahman, from the top of Tower Hill.

Adam-ondi-Ahman is important to Latter-day Saints for at least two reasons. As Joseph's revelation makes clear, it will be the site of a future meeting involving Adam and "his people" (D&C 116:1). Christ will also be present at this meeting, during which he will receive "dominion, and glory, and a kingdom, that all people, nations, and languages, should serve him" (Daniel 7:14).

But the area is also sacred for what happened there in the distant past. Through revelation, Joseph had learned earlier that "three years previous to the death of Adam, he called Seth, Enos, Cainan, Mahalaleel, Jared, Enoch, and Methuselah, who were all high priests, with the residue of his posterity who were righteous, into the valley of Adam-ondi-Ahman, and there bestowed upon them his last blessing." The Lord appeared and "administered comfort unto Adam," after which Adam "stood up in the midst of the congregation; and notwithstanding he was bowed down with age, being full of the Holy Ghost, predicted whatsoever should befall his posterity unto the latest generation" (D&C 107:53–56).

For all its storied past and future glory, Adam-ondi-Ahman witnessed little more than heartache and persecution for the Saints living there in 1838. To be sure, prospects there for the Church initially looked bright. During his visit in May, for example, Joseph designated the area north and west of Tower Hill as the site for a full-blown city, and he organized a stake there the following month. Some four hundred Latter-day Saints moved to the area over the course of the summer and fall, including scores newly arrived in Missouri from Kirtland and Canada. A temple site was even dedicated.

Missourians' resentment over the Mormons' expansion beyond the borders of Caldwell County boiled over into active persecution against Church members in the area.

By October, however, Missourians' resentment over the Mormons' expansion beyond the borders of Caldwell County boiled over into active persecution against Church members in the area, with men gathering "from all the upper counties to join the mob to the number of several hundreds," Albert Rockwood remembered. "They continued to encamp in various places for several miles round Adam-ondi-Ahman for about two weeks, taking some prisoners, robbing and insulting in various ways many of the brethren, and driving many from their homes."[13]

Most of the persecution had been directed toward Saints living in isolated areas in the county; by October residents of Adam-ondi-Ahman itself were threatened. Men from Far West administered what aid they could, with Joseph even organizing an impromptu snowball fight at one point to boost morale. Saints in the area held several meetings in Lyman Wight's second cabin after the issuance of the extermination order and Joseph's capture at Far West, and they joined other Church members in fleeing the state during the winter of 1838–39.

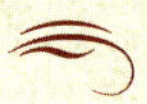

Church members at Adam-ondi-Ahman suffered tremendous loss in the fall of 1838, but overall they did not fare as badly as others. On October 24, for example, thirty-five members of the Ray County militia, under the command of Samuel Bogart, took three Latter-day Saints—Nathan Pinkham Jr., William Seely, and Addison Green—hostage in northern Ray County. When reports reached Far West that Bogart planned to execute the three men the following morning, Elias Higbee, the Mormon judge of Caldwell County, sent Elder David W. Patten and sixty men to rescue the hostages. Just as it was beginning to get light on the morning of October 25, Patten and his men met Bogart's picket guard on the road a quarter mile from Bogart's camp on the east bank of Crooked River. Following a brief exchange of gunfire with the guard in which Patrick Obanion, a non-Mormon guide for Patten's men, was wounded, the Saints advanced upon the Missourians, who were crouched under the

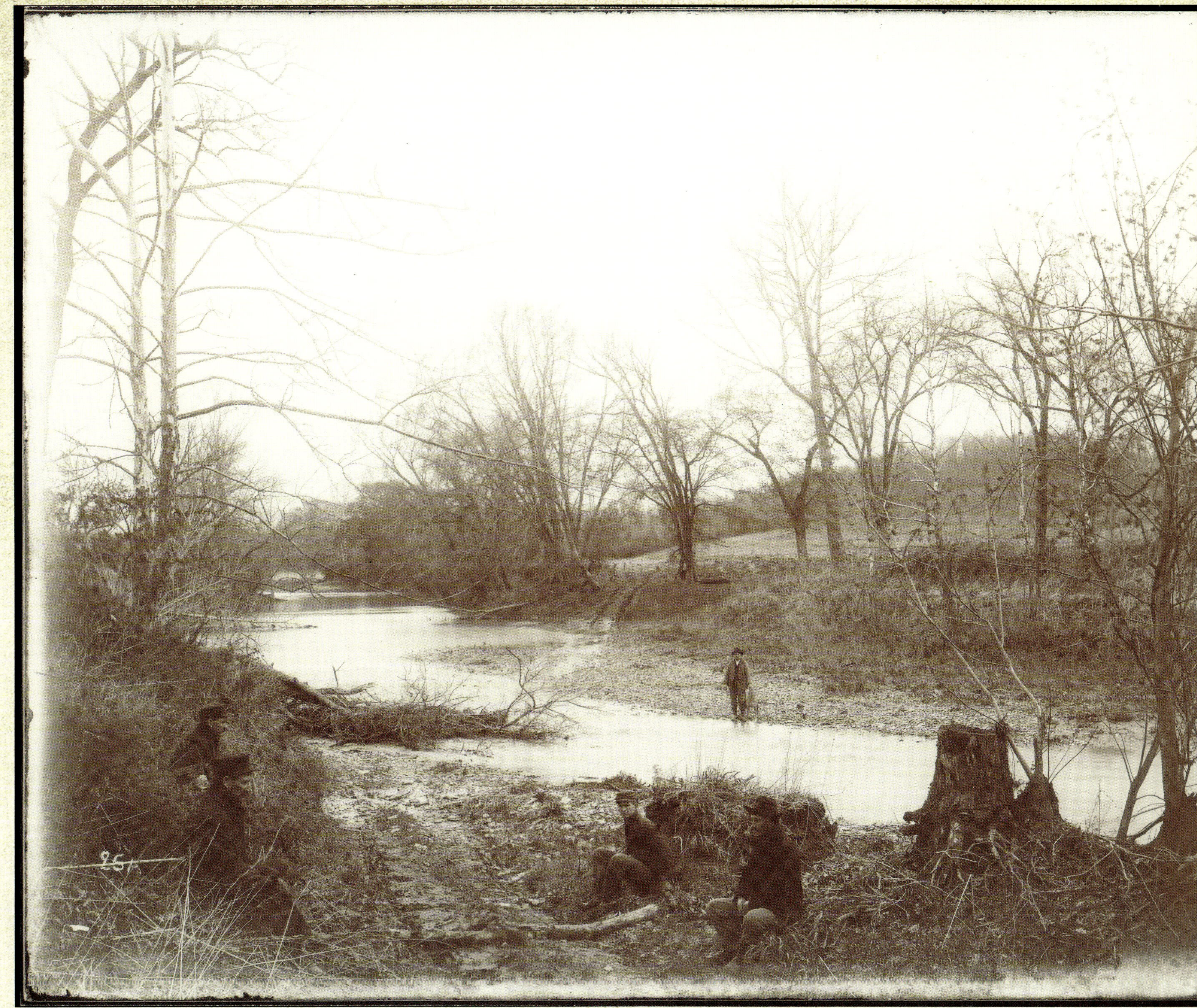

Battleground site on Crooked River, Missouri, May 15, 1907, Anderson Collection, LDS Church History Library, Salt Lake City, Utah.

creek's four-foot-high bank and almost entirely hidden from view.[14] In the battle that followed, Elder Parley P. Pratt recalled, "the whole wilderness seemed one continued echo of the report of the deadly rifle."[15]

Unable to drive Bogart's men from their position with gunfire alone, Patten ordered his men to charge. The show of force worked, with most of the Missourians firing their guns and fleeing in the face of the advancing Mormons. Two of Bogart's men, however, lingered behind for a time before running, with Patten and Charles C. Rich in close pursuit. The man Patten

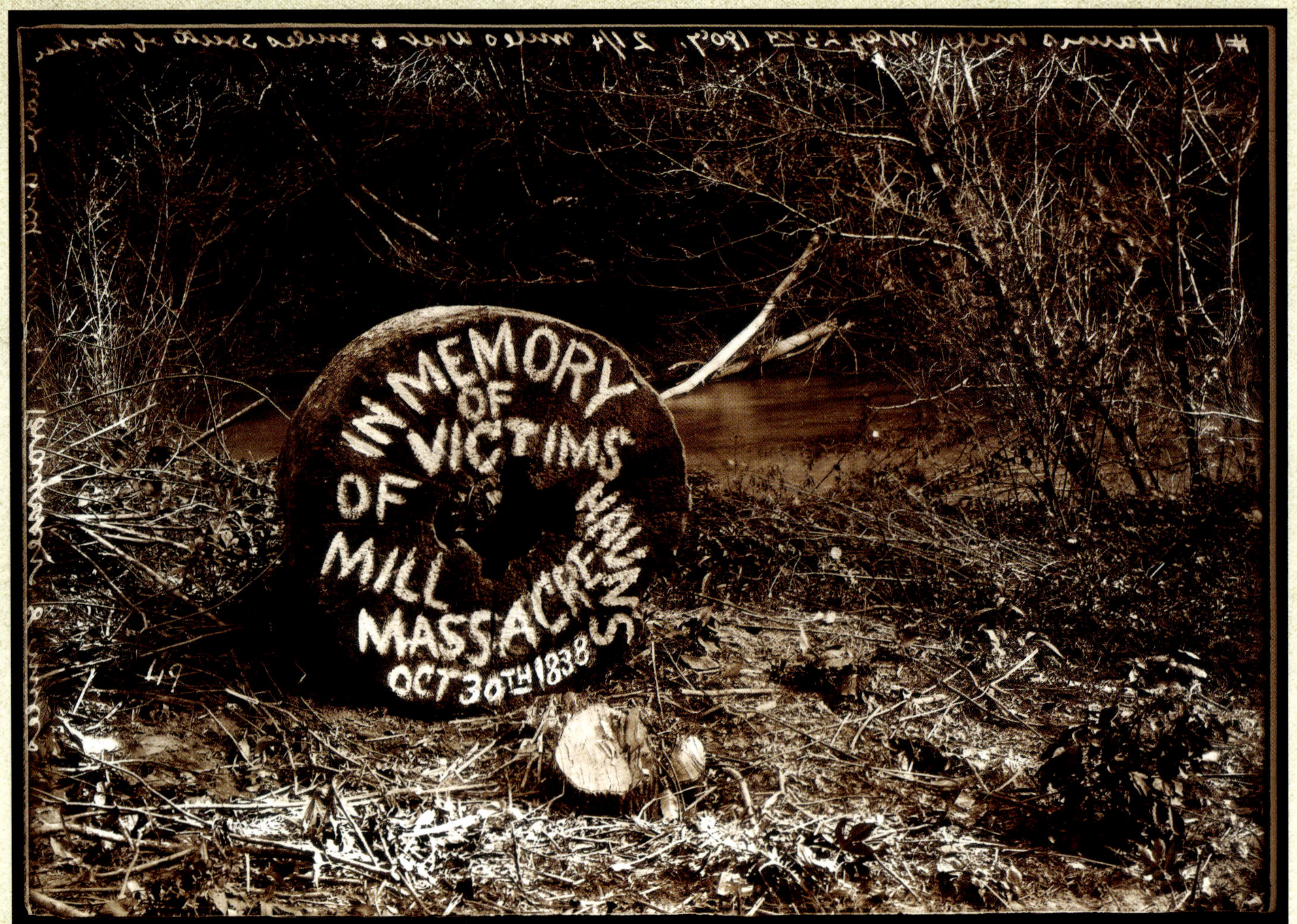

Millstone at Haun's Mill, Missouri, May 23, 1907, Anderson Collection, LDS Church History Library, Salt Lake City, Utah.

was chasing turned and fired at Patten, whose white coat made an excellent target in the predawn light. Patten fell, wounded in his lower abdomen, while his men continued their charge under Rich's direction. The attack ended shortly afterward, when Rich and the others determined that the three hostages had managed to escape the Missourians in the confusion of their flight.[16]

In all, nine of Patten's men, including himself, were wounded at the Battle of Crooked River. A tenth, Gideon Carter, was killed outright during the battle, "his face . . . so marred and disfigured with wounds and blood," Pratt wrote later, "that I did not recognize him."[17] Although most of the wounded eventually fully recovered, James Hendricks, who had been shot in the neck, suffered effects of his injury for the rest of his life. Patten and Obanion, the non-Mormon guide who had been wounded by the picket guard, both died from their wounds—Patten about four that afternoon, Obanion shortly afterward.[18] It was the first time an apostle had been killed in this dispensation.

The effects of the battle, however, would be felt far beyond the families of the men who had been wounded or killed. Only one Missourian, Moses Rowland, had been killed in the battle, but the report that reached Governor

Before most Church members heard of the extermination order, another tragedy struck the Missouri Saints.

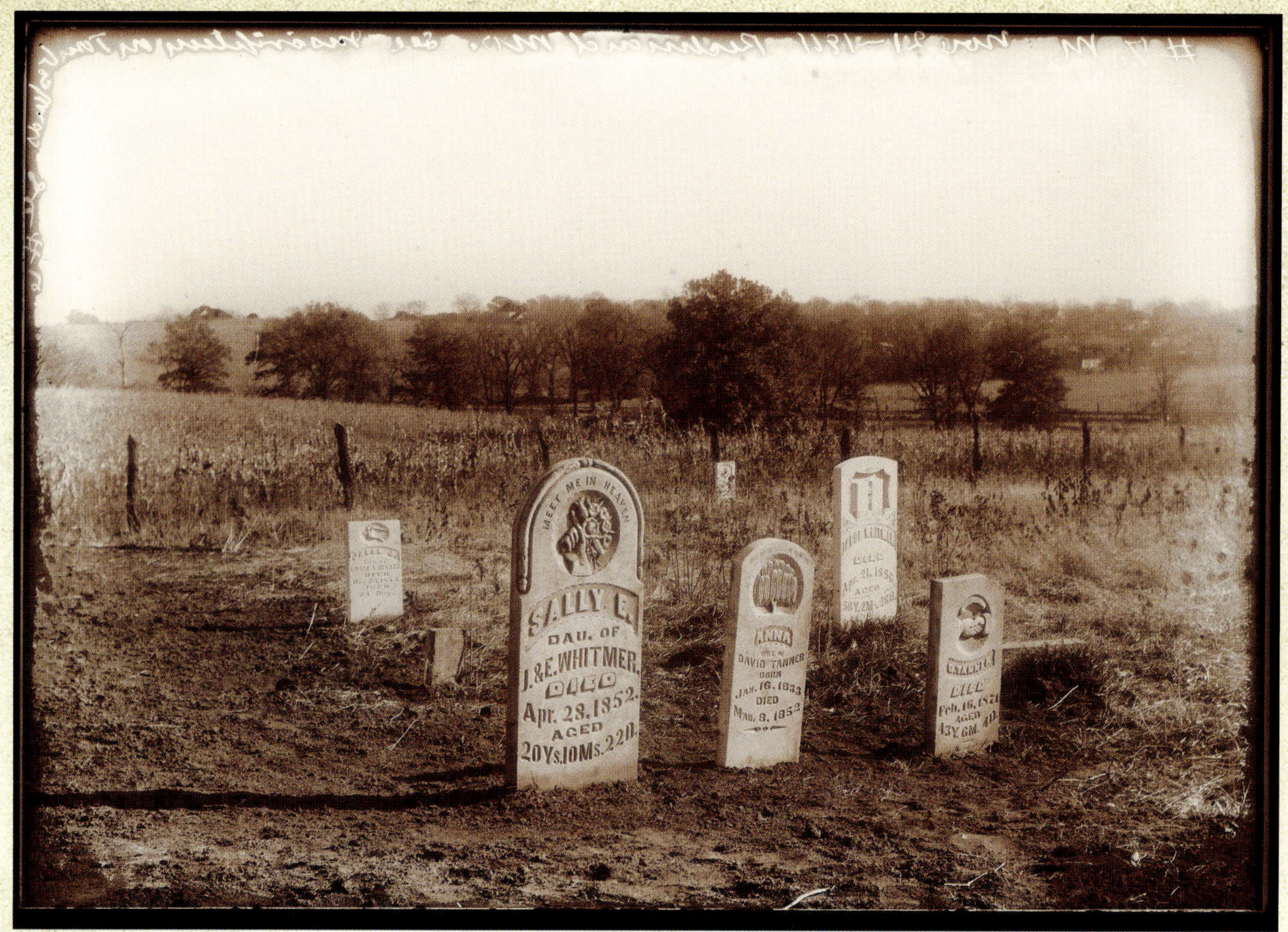

Tombstone of Jacob Whitmer (second row, right), Pioneer Cemetery, Richmond, Missouri, May 10, 1907, Anderson Collection, LDS Church History Library, Salt Lake City, Utah.

Boggs had the Mormons massacring fifty to sixty Missourians on the banks of the river.[19] Convinced from what he had heard that the Mormons were declaring war against the people of Missouri, Boggs issued his extermination order on October 27, thereby setting in motion the events that would culminate in the incarceration of Joseph Smith in Liberty Jail and the forced expulsion of thousands of Latter-day Saints from Missouri. In a very real sense, Anderson's photograph of Crooked River is a picture of the beginning of some of the Church's darkest days.

Before most Church members heard of the extermination order, however, another tragedy struck the Missouri Saints. Late in the afternoon of October 30, a group of more than two hundred Missourians attacked the Saints living at Haun's Mill, on Shoal Creek in Caldwell County. Angered, apparently, at Mormon efforts to rid Daviess County of hostile Missourians earlier in the month, the Missourians had first robbed the Saints in the area of their guns and then, over the course of several days, made overtures of peace toward them.[20] As a result, the small group at Haun's Mill—some of whom had just arrived from Kirtland—were caught completely off guard by the attack.

"More than three-fourths of the day had passed in tranquility," remembered Joseph Young. "I think there was no individual of our company that was apprised of the sudden and awful fate that hung over our heads like an overwhelming torrent. . . . The banks of Shoal creek on either side teemed with children sporting and playing, while their mothers were engaged in domestic employments, and their fathers employed in guarding the mills and other property, while others were engaged in gathering in their crops."[21]

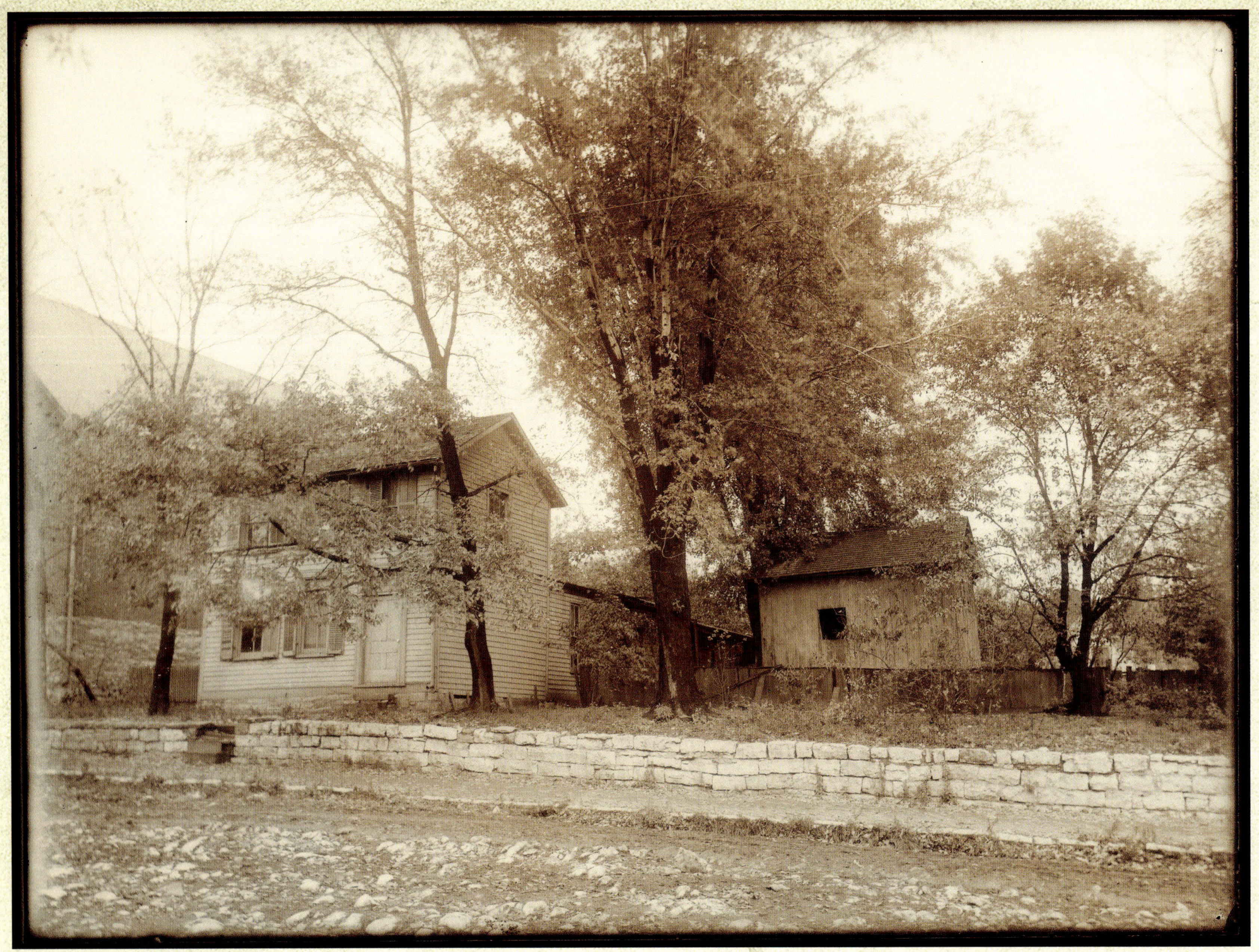

Home of David and Julia Ann Whitmer, Richmond, Missouri, probably May 1907, Anderson Collection, LDS Church History Library, Salt Lake City, Utah.

Young, who had just arrived, was holding his baby in a cabin when the Missourians, led by Thomas Jennings of Livingston County, rode into the settlement and began shooting. After the initial volley, most of the shots were directed toward the settlement's blacksmith shop, where many of the men and some of the children had fled for safety. Riding up to the shop, the Missourians shot at those inside, at point-blank range, through the chinks between the logs. Those who fled into the woods, including Joseph Young, also came under fire. The mob then fell to robbing the Saints' houses and wagons, driving off their teams, and even stripping some of the dead of their clothing.

No one was spared in the attack, including the aged and the very young. Thomas McBride, for example, born in 1776, was shot with his own gun after he gave it up; then one of the mob mutilated his body with a corn cutter. Similarly, nine-year-old Sardius Smith was killed while begging for his life after one of the mob found him hiding under the bellows in the blacksmith shop. His younger brother, Alma, who had been shot in the thigh, escaped a similar fate by pretending to be dead—a tactic employed by at least two men, William Champlin and Jacob Foutz.[22] In all, seventeen Latter-day Saints were killed in the attack. Another fourteen were wounded. These included at least one woman, Mary Stedwell, who had been shot through the hand, and Isaac Leany, who counted twenty-seven bullet holes in his shirt, eight of them from bullets that went through his body.[23] Fearing that the mob would return, the survivors buried the dead the next morning in a single mass grave, using a large "vault in the ground, formerly intended for a well."[24] The settlement was abandoned shortly afterward and fell into oblivion after the Saints left Missouri. The millstone Anderson found and photographed in May 1907, and on which he memorialized the Saints who had been killed there, is a poignant reminder of the worst single act of violence committed against members of the Church in this dispensation.

Not everyone we identify with the Restoration left Missouri with the Saints in the early months of 1839. Following their apostasy in 1838, for example, Jacob and David Whitmer lived in the Richmond area until their deaths in 1856 and 1888, respectively. Jacob, a shoemaker, farmed during the summers and worked in his shop during the winter; David ran a livery stable and was elected mayor of Richmond in 1867. Both had been instrumental in the coming forth of the Book of Mormon—David as one of the Three Witnesses, Jacob as one of the Eight Witnesses. Both remained true to their testimony of the book despite their estrangement from the Church.

Outliving all of the other witnesses of the Book of Mormon, David especially had opportunity to reiterate his experience with the plates; records and accounts of more than fifty interviews with him survive. Whitmer's Richmond home, captured in Anderson's photograph, served as the setting for many of these interviews. In each of them, David emphasized the absolute, physical reality of his experience—an insistence more than one of his non-Mormon neighbors found inconsistent with his otherwise unimpeachable character. One Latter-day Saint who visited David Whitmer was Angus Cannon, a younger brother of George Q. Cannon. He recalled that David Whitmer, even on his deathbed, "as helpless as a child," managed to raise his hand and declare that "if God ever uttered a truth, the testimony I now bear is true. I did see the angel of God, and I beheld the glory of the Lord, and he declared the record true."[25] Although many Saints today may identify Missouri with mobs and persecution, we need to remember that Missouri is also the place where the last testimony ever borne in mortality by one of the Three Witnesses of the Book of Mormon was given.

6

Illinois

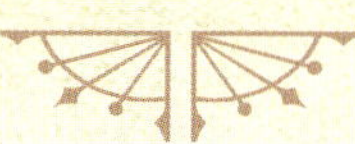

George Edward Anderson followed in the footsteps of Joseph Smith and the early Saints when he left Missouri, eventually crossing the Mississippi River to Illinois on May 1, 1907.[1] On the following day he noted in a small pocket diary, "Found [LDS missionaries] Sister Ida Alleman and Sister Bennion soon after 6:45 . . . this morning and, with them, visited the most interesting points—old homes of the Saints, the Prophet's home, temple ground. In the afternoon, made views of the most prominent places."[2]

Anderson continued documenting with his camera what he saw in Nauvoo and Carthage during the next six days. These unforgettable images augment the words preserved in Nauvoo-period diaries, letters, and later reminiscences of the Latter-day Saints. Together, the original glass plates and the original pen and paper documents provide a window into the world that existed when the people of God built their city on the banks of the Mississippi River between 1839 and 1846.

> George Edward Anderson followed in the footsteps of Joseph Smith and the early Saints, crossing the Mississippi River to Illinois.

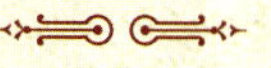

The Latter-day Saint winter exodus from Missouri in 1838–39 dashed their dreams and hopes of building cities of faith and peace, along with temples, in the land they believed had a sacred past and future (D&C 107:53–57; 116). As the Saints, under the direction of Brigham Young, made their way to safety in Illinois and Iowa, Joseph Smith and several other Church leaders remained behind in Missouri imprisoned in dark, dank jails during that winter.

Eventually, Joseph and his fellow prisoners were allowed to escape incarceration, and they found a large body of Saints waiting patiently for the Prophet in Quincy, Adams County, Illinois, in the spring of 1839. Within a short time, Joseph identified a new Church headquarters site several miles north of Quincy—the future Nauvoo. This new gathering place, "the cornerstone" appointed "for Zion" (D&C 124:23), was the destination of thousands of Latter-day Saints.

The city of Nauvoo did not resemble precisely the typical frontier settlements one would expect at this time in American history. As Carol Cornwall Madsen has observed, "Nauvoo reflected a family settlement pattern, the ratio of women and men nearly at parity."[3] The faithful and dedicated men, women, and children

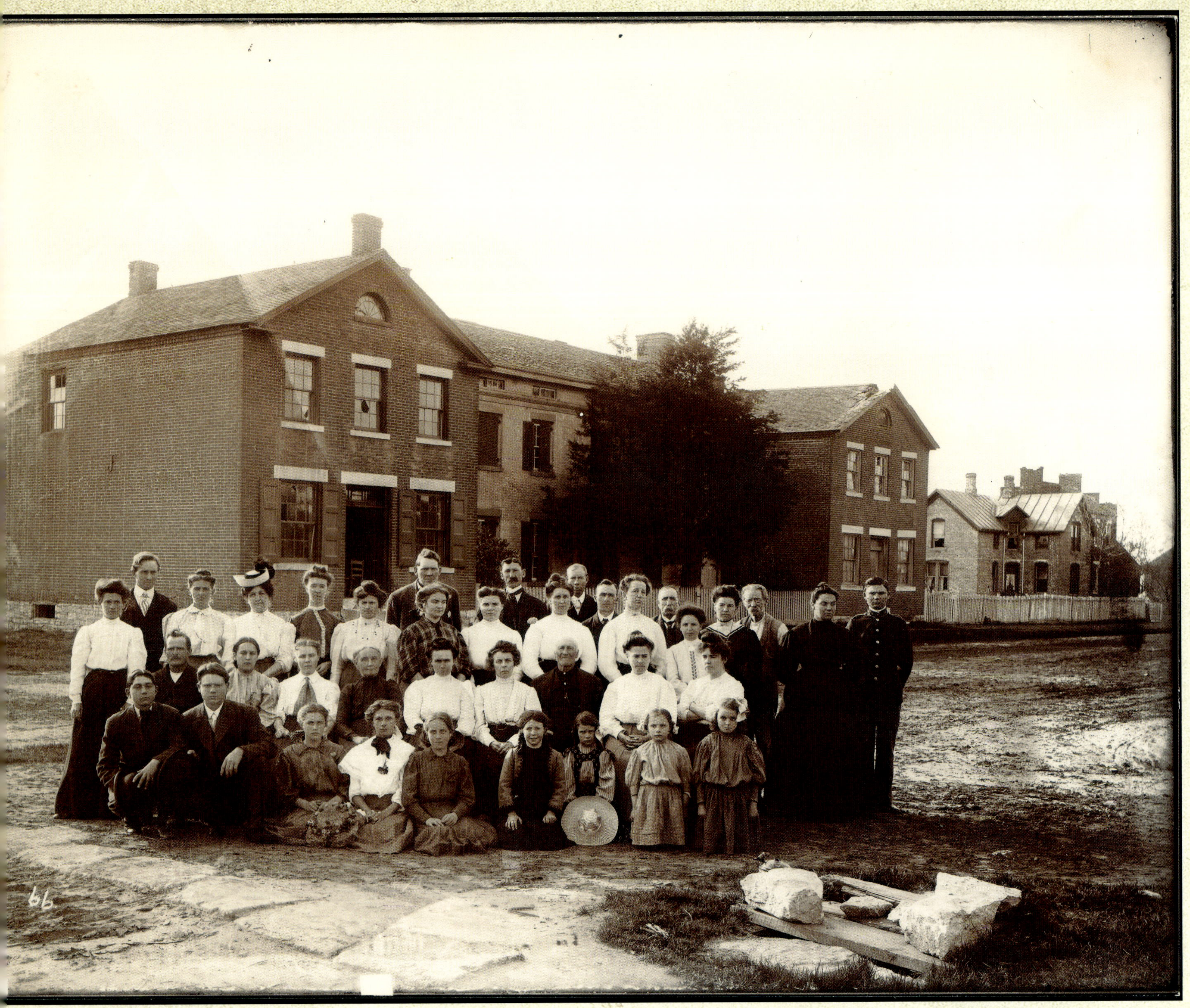

Missionaries and local Latter-day Saints in front of the printing office, the Ivins-Smith-Taylor home, and the post office, Nauvoo, Illinois, May 2, 1907, Anderson Collection, LDS Church History Library, Salt Lake City, Utah.

who gathered to western Illinois came from Canada, the British Isles, and all over the United States (north, east, and south) to help build the city and the temple and to hear the Prophet of the Lord speak the words of eternal life.[4] Among them were divorced and abandoned single men and women—work-hardened laborers who grew up on rural farmsteads or in the industrial towns and cities of England, where grinding poverty had left them without hope. Free blacks and formerly

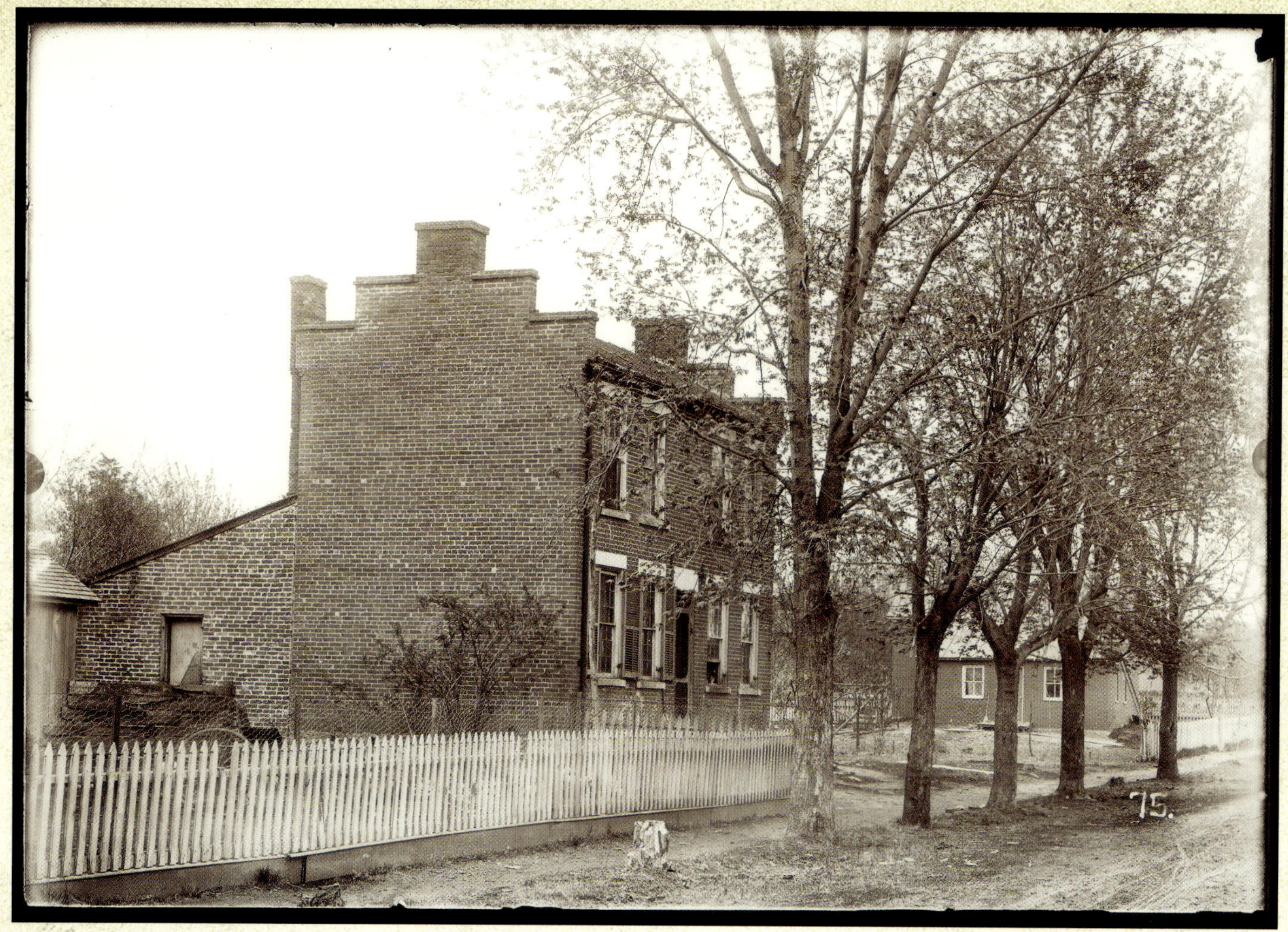

Home of John D. and Agatha Woolsey Lee, Nauvoo, Illinois, May 1907, Anderson Collection, L. Tom Perry Special Collections, Brigham Young University, Provo, Utah.

indentured white servants also came to Nauvoo, where they mingled with all classes of people who lived in or visited the city of the Saints.

As a river town on the Mississippi, Nauvoo had its share of counterfeiters, gamblers, drunkards, and other disreputable people hovering on the edge of polite society. People gathered with the Saints from both nonreligious and religious backgrounds, including Jews, Catholics, and Protestants of all stripes. The citizens of Nauvoo included skilled artisans and common laborers. Some of them were accomplished, offering piano, painting, and drama lessons. Others were inventors and practitioners of newly developed technologies, including photography. The message of the gospel had drawn in all kinds of fish (Matthew 13:47).

The effects of the Missouri persecutions and the malaria-infested swamps along the Mississippi River took a heavy toll upon men, women, and children during the first two years of settlement. Many died as family members watched their love ones fade away, both old and young. "It seems almost impossible," wrote Nancy Tracey, "to raise a child in Nauvoo."[5]

Nevertheless, through tremendous exertion, faith, and resolve, the Saints transformed a promontory that jutted out from the eastern banks of the Mississippi River, known as the flats, into a large, thriving city of more than eleven thousand inhabitants. Approximately two thousand whitewashed log, wood-frame, and brick homes were built. Additionally, a number of businesses and shops dotted the expanding environs of Nauvoo. The focus of this unique religious community, however, was a beautiful white limestone temple rising majestically on the bluff overlooking the area.

Nauvoo's rapid growth and unique religious orientation elicited economic jealousy, political alarm, and religious bigotry from some of its neighbors. Eventually, a number of citizens in Hancock County, including some of the most influential men, organized an anti-Mormon party that utilized every possible means, including extralegal acts, to force the Saints from their beautiful city in 1846.

By the end of the Nauvoo period, the Church itself had also been transformed. The basic doctrines of faith in Jesus Christ and repentance, combined with the central truth of the Atonement and reconciliation with God through the Son—reaffirmed in the revealed message of the Restoration—remained the foundation of Latter-day Saint belief. During the five-year period from 1839 to 1844, the Lord continued to make known his word and will to the Prophet Joseph Smith in Nauvoo. And during this significant doctrinal period, the Lord gave the Church ordinances, principles, and eternal truths "which have been kept hid from before the foundation of the world, things that pertain to the dispensation of the fulness of times" (D&C 124:41).

From Joseph Smith's death in 1844 through the exodus in 1846, the Twelve Apostles attempted to fulfill Joseph's measures as they bore "off this Church and Kingdom of God before heaven and earth, and before God, angels and men."[6]

Adding to the sacred ordinances established in the New York and Ohio periods—baptism, the sacrament, priesthood ordinations, and patriarchal blessings—the Lord introduced the fulness of temple worship, including proxy baptisms, endowments, and sealings (eternal marriage).

Adding to the sacred ordinances established in New York and Ohio, the Lord introduced the fulness of temple worship, including proxy baptisms, endowments, and sealings.

In January 1841, in Nauvoo, the Prophet received section 124, the longest revelation in the Doctrine and Covenants. Historian Steven C. Harper asserts, "The revelation oriented [Joseph Smith's] life and that of the Church."[7] It begins, "Verily, thus saith the Lord unto you, my servant Joseph Smith, I am well pleased with your offering and acknowledgments, which you have made; for unto this end have I raised you up, that I might show forth my wisdom through the weak things of the earth" (D&C 124:1).

Although section 124 contains specific commandments on a variety of issues, it also identifies four general duties. First, Church leaders were commanded to prepare "a solemn proclamation" (v. 2).[8] Second, the Saints were commanded to build a hotel in Nauvoo, the Nauvoo House, to provide lodging for visitors (v. 23).[9] Third, the revelation called for the reorganization of the priesthood quorums that had been depleted by death and by apostasy in Ohio and Missouri (vv. 123–43). Fourth, the revelation commanded the Saints to "build a house to my name, for the Most High to dwell therein" (v. 27).[10]

The Lord continued: "Verily I say unto you, that your anointings and your washings, and your baptisms for the dead, and your solemn assemblies, and your memorials for your sacrifices by the sons of Levi, and for your oracles in your most holy places wherein you receive conversations, and your statutes and judgments, for the beginning of the

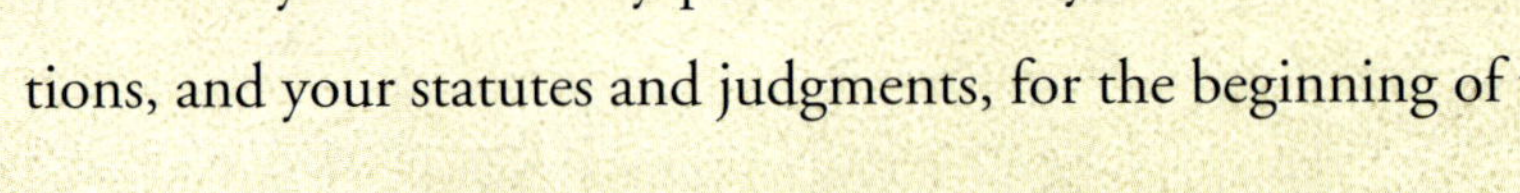

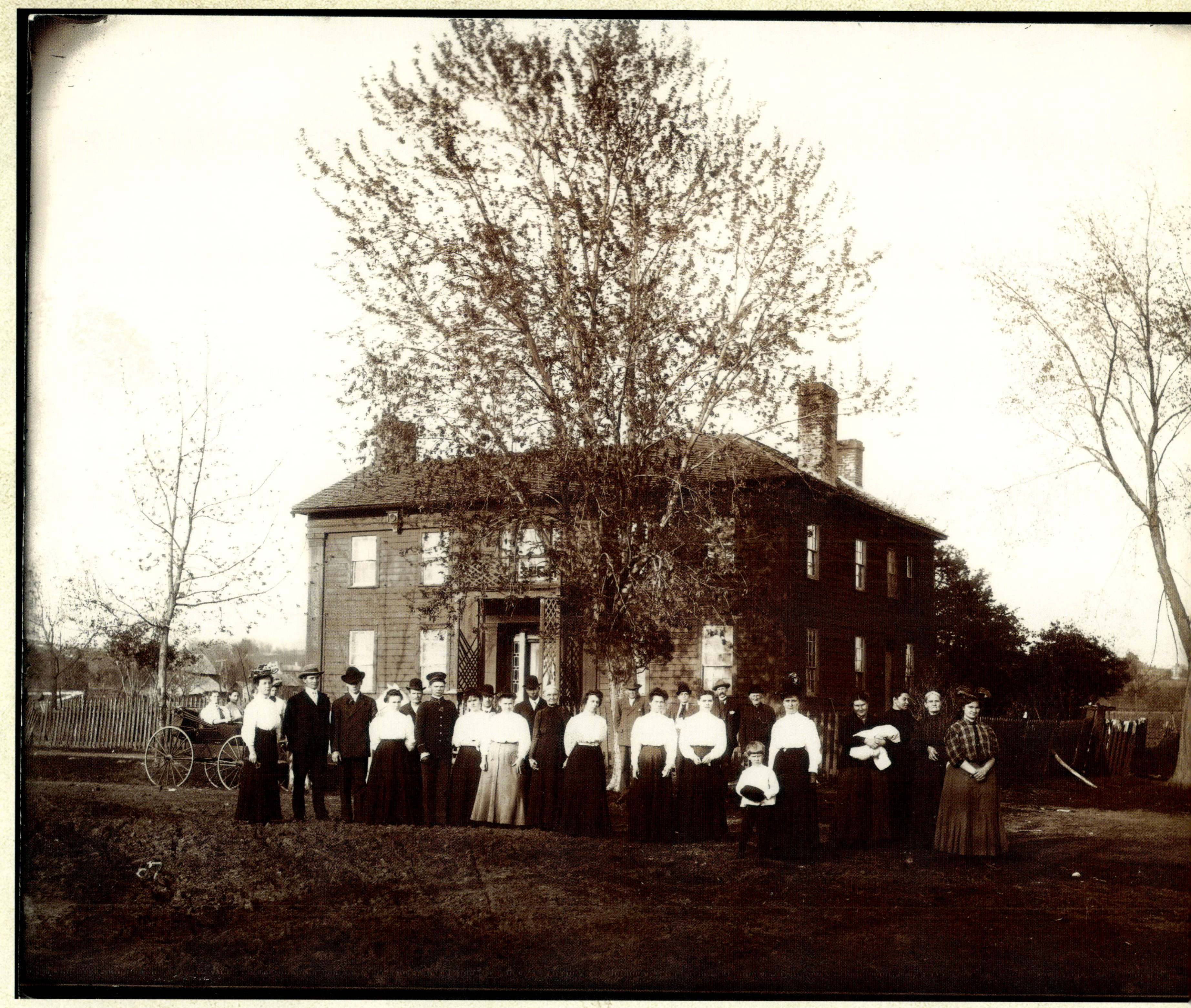

Home of Joseph and Emma Smith (Mansion House), Nauvoo, Illinois, May 2, 1907, Anderson Collection, LDS Church History Library, Salt Lake City, Utah.

revelations and foundation of Zion, and for the glory, honor, and endowment of all her municipals, are ordained by the ordinance of my holy house, which my people are always commanded to build unto my holy name" (v. 39).

Like the Kirtland Temple, the Nauvoo Temple was planned as a multiuse building. The ground floor was a general assembly room (used much like a modern chapel or a stake center). The second floor was planned for education

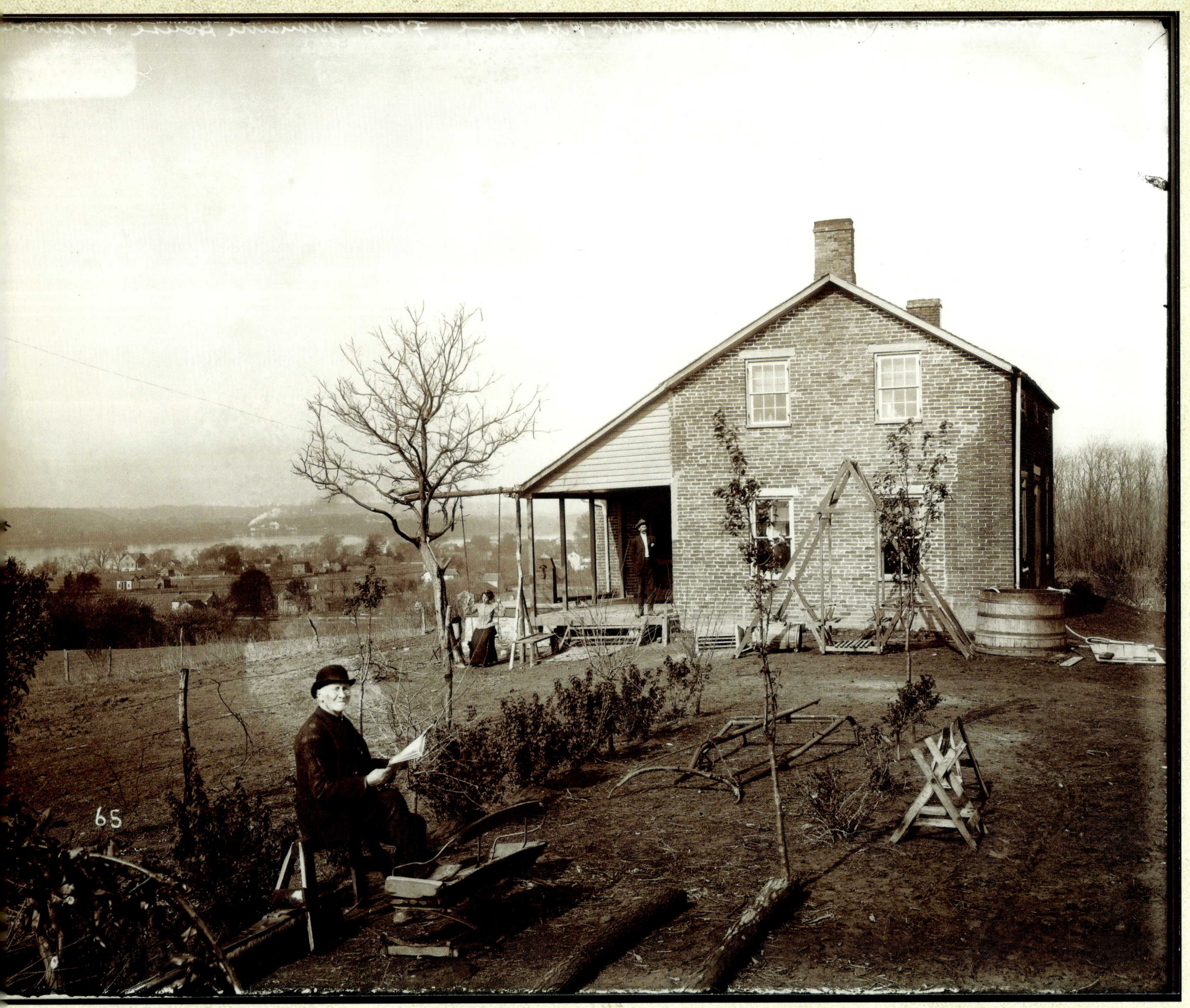

Home of Charles and Emma Davidson Pitt, recently baptized Church members, Nauvoo, Illinois, May 4, 1907, Anderson Collection, LDS Church History Library, Salt Lake City, Utah.

and training (like buildings on Brigham Young University campuses, seminary and institute buildings, and the buildings at missionary training center complexes). The attic was designed for the performing of temple ordinances (as in temples today), and an administrative office was built for administrative duties (like the Church Administration Building in Salt Lake City).

The Nauvoo Temple (measuring 128 feet by 88 feet and with a tower reaching 165 feet) was much larger than the Kirtland Temple (measuring 79 feet by 59 feet and with a tower reaching

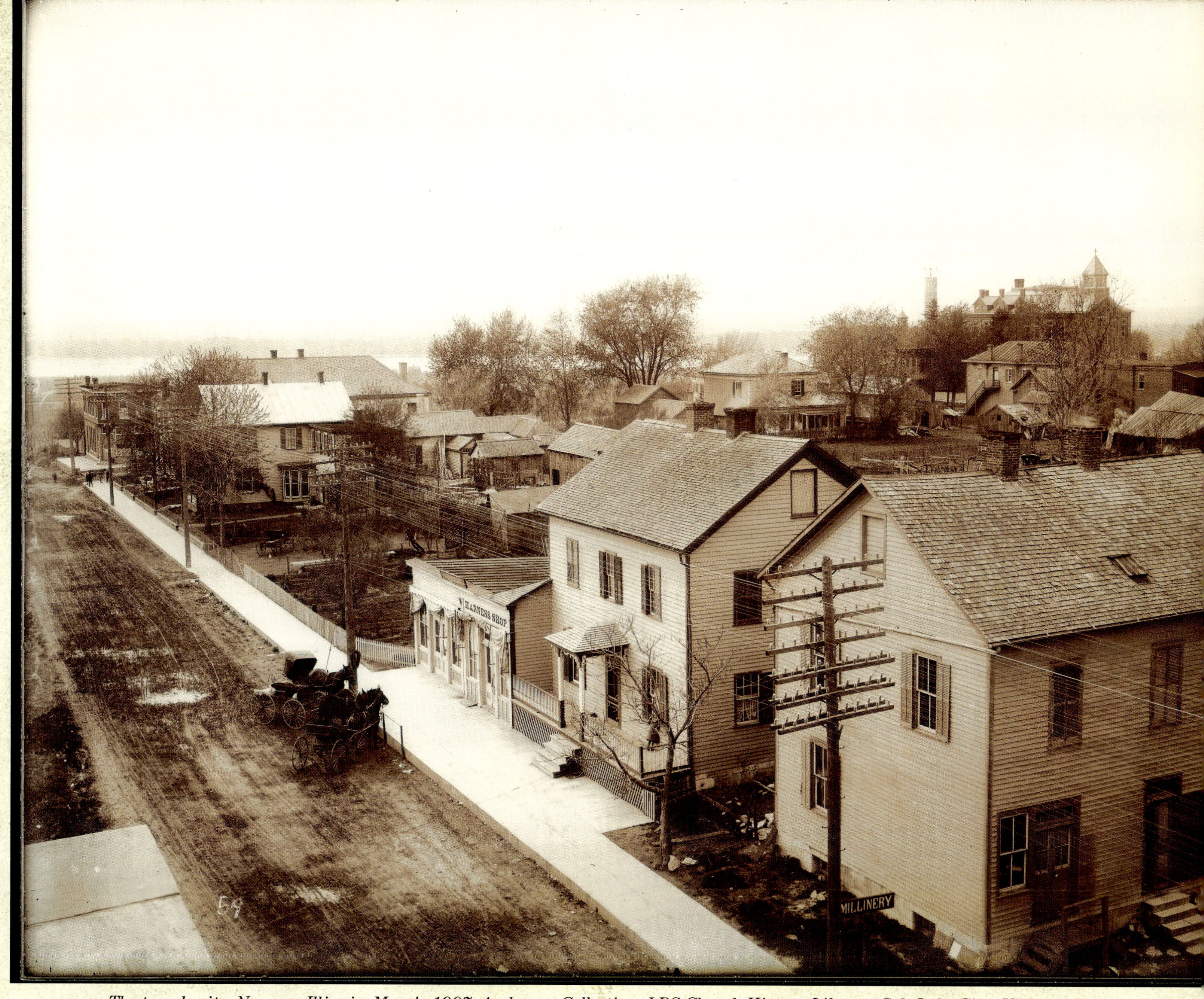

The temple site, Nauvoo, Illinois, May 4, 1907, Anderson Collection, LDS Church History Library, Salt Lake City, Utah.

110 feet). Additionally, the Nauvoo Temple was different in other ways. For example, it had a full basement for a baptismal font. The font was primarily used for baptisms for the dead. Locating the font in the basement reminded the Saints of the grave, adding to the rich symbolism of this temple. Unlike the earlier temple, the Nauvoo Temple exterior displayed symbolic features, including a weathervane prominently displaying the figure of the angel Moroni dressed in sacred clothing—a cap and flowing robe, a square and compass, as well as starstones, moonstones, and sunstones, symbolism preserved in later temples.[11]

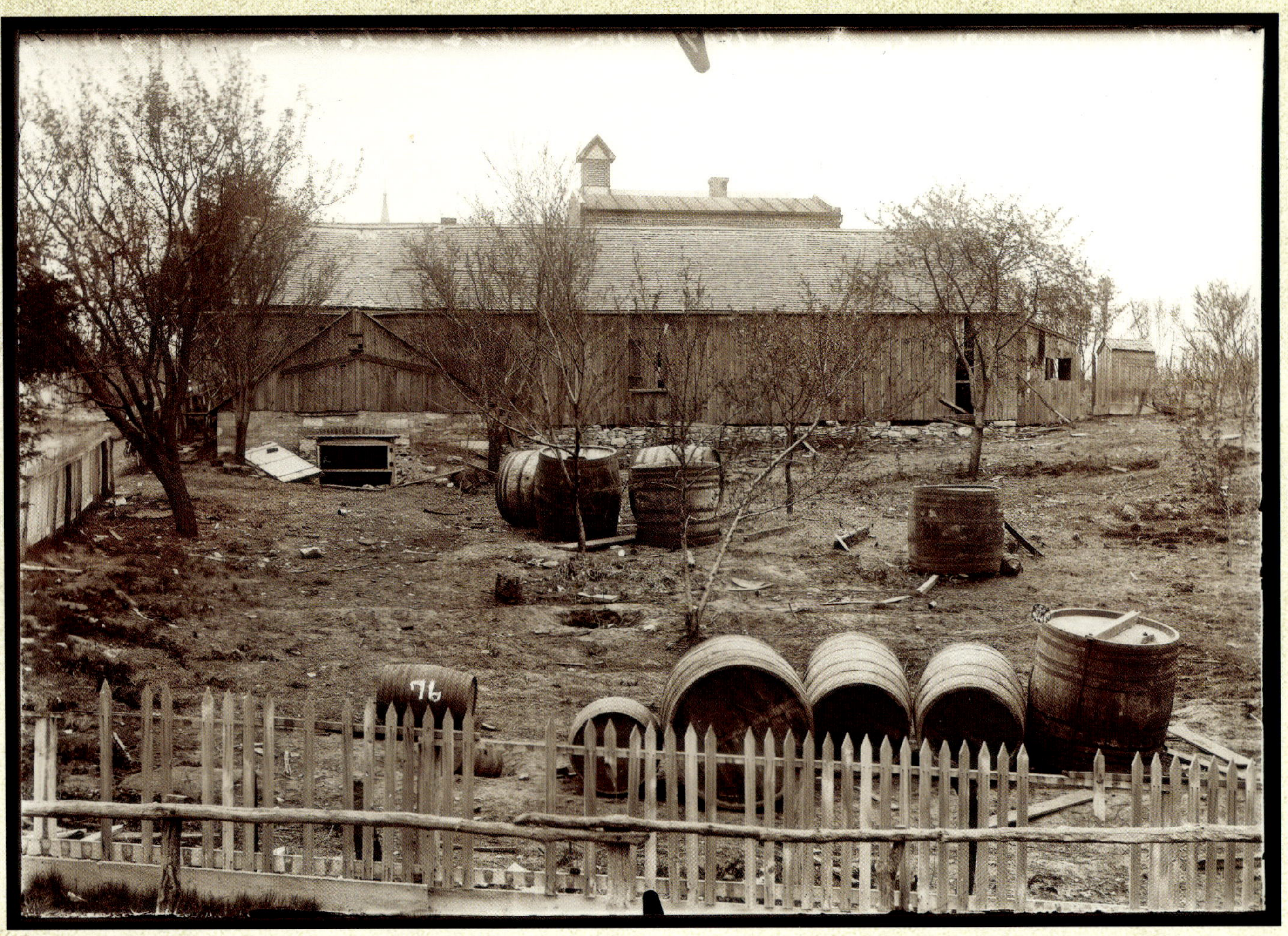

Wine cellar lot with Nauvoo Temple property behind the buildings, Nauvoo, Illinois, May 4, 1907, Anderson Collection, LDS Church History Library, Salt Lake City, Utah.

The Lord told Joseph Smith that he would provide the Saints a great blessing, "even the fulness of the priesthood" (D&C 124:28), if they did as the Lord commanded. Shortly after the January 19, 1841, revelation was received, the Lord revealed the temple ordinances that were necessary to prepare the Saints to receive the fulness of the priesthood. Basing his command on a divinely appointed time frame, the Lord asked Joseph to begin this work with a small, select group of men and women before the temple was completed. Later, these Saints assisted the general body of the Church to receive these same blessings in the Nauvoo Temple from December 1845 to February 1846.

The Prophet explained that there are "certain signs & words . . . which cannot be revealed to the Elders till the Temple is completed.—The rich can only get them in the Temple. The poor may get them on the mountain top as did Moses."[12] Joseph Smith dedicated a few upper rooms in Nauvoo (in the Homestead, the Mansion House, and the Red Brick Store) to perform these sacred ordinances to the select group of men and women.

As he did in the time immediately before the completion of the Kirtland Temple in 1836, Joseph Smith began to prepare the Saints to receive blessings in the Nauvoo Temple. For example, during a Relief Society meeting, the Prophet "gave a lecture on the Priesthood, showing how the sisters would come in possession of the privileges, blessings and gifts of the Priesthood."[13] He then "exhorted the sisters always to concentrate their faith and prayers for, and place confidence in their

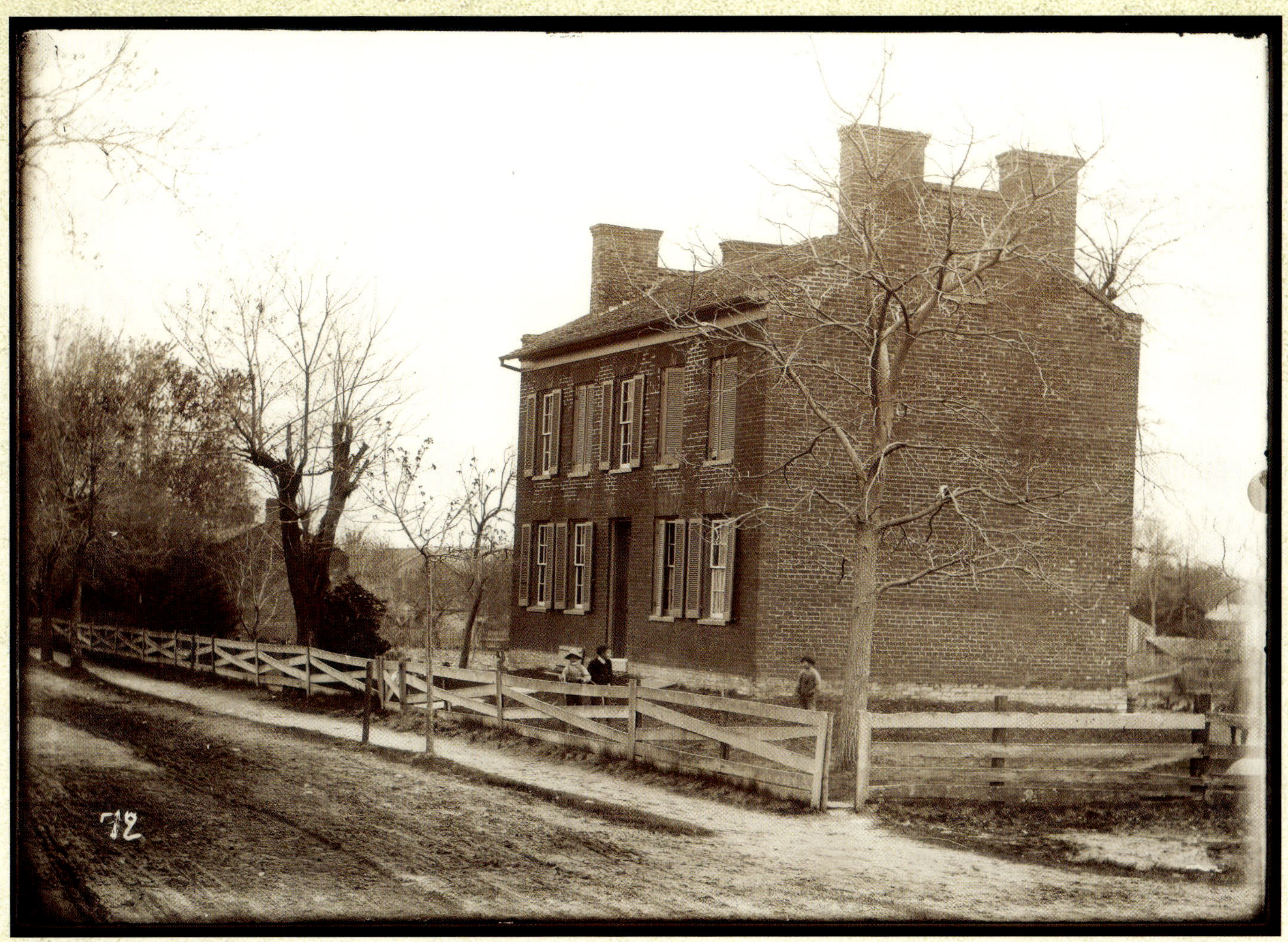

Home of Wilford and Phoebe Carter Woodruff, Nauvoo, Illinois, May 1907, Anderson Collection, L. Tom Perry Special Collections, Brigham Young University, Provo, Utah.

husbands, whom God has appointed for them to honor, and in those faithful men whom God has placed at the head of the Church to lead His people; that we should arm and sustain them with our prayers; for the keys of the kingdom are about to be given to them [Church leaders], that they may be able to detect everything false."[14]

Joseph indicated that the "keys of the Priesthood" (presumably, the temple endowment keys) would be given to members of the Church, both men and women. The Prophet "spoke of delivering the keys of the Priesthood to the Church, and said that the faithful members of the Relief Society should receive them in connection with their husbands, that the Saints whose integrity has been tried and proved faithful, might know how to ask the Lord and receive an answer."[15]

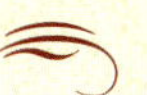

On May 4, 1842, six days following this Relief Society meeting in 1842, nine Church members met in the upper room of Joseph's Red Brick Store on Water Street in a special meeting and received their temple blessings from Joseph. They became the first in this dispensation to receive their "washings, anointing, endowments, and the communication of keys pertaining to the Aaronic Priesthood, and so on to the highest order of the Melchisedek Priesthood, setting forth the order pertaining to the Ancient of Days, and all those plans and principles by which any one is enabled to secure the fullness of those blessings which have been prepared for the Church of the First Born, and come up and abide in the presence of the Eloheim in the eternal worlds."[16]

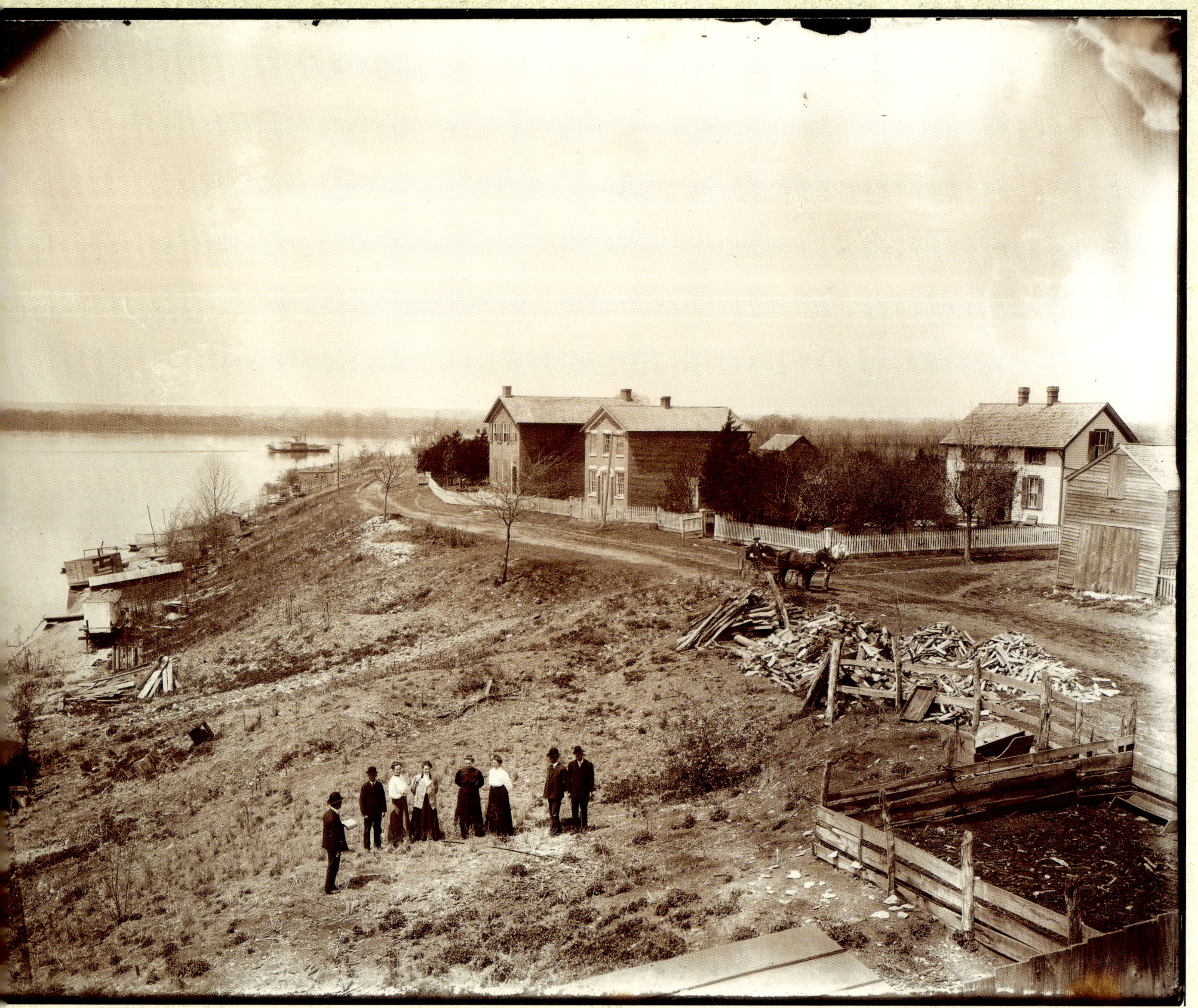

Homes of Jonathan Wright and Aaron Johnson, Water Street, Nauvoo, Illinois, May 4, 1907, Anderson Collection, L. Tom Perry Special Collections, Brigham Young University, Provo, Utah.

Bishop Newel K. Whitney spoke to some of the women of the Relief Society in Nauvoo a few weeks after he received his endowment: "Rejoice while contemplating the blessings which will be poured out on the heads of the Saints. God has many precious things to bestow, ever to our astonishment, if we are faithful." The society's secretary noted that Bishop Whitney then "rejoiced at the formation of the society, that we might improve our talents and . . . prepare for those blessings which God is soon to bestow upon us."[17]

Members of the Quorum of the Twelve Apostles played a

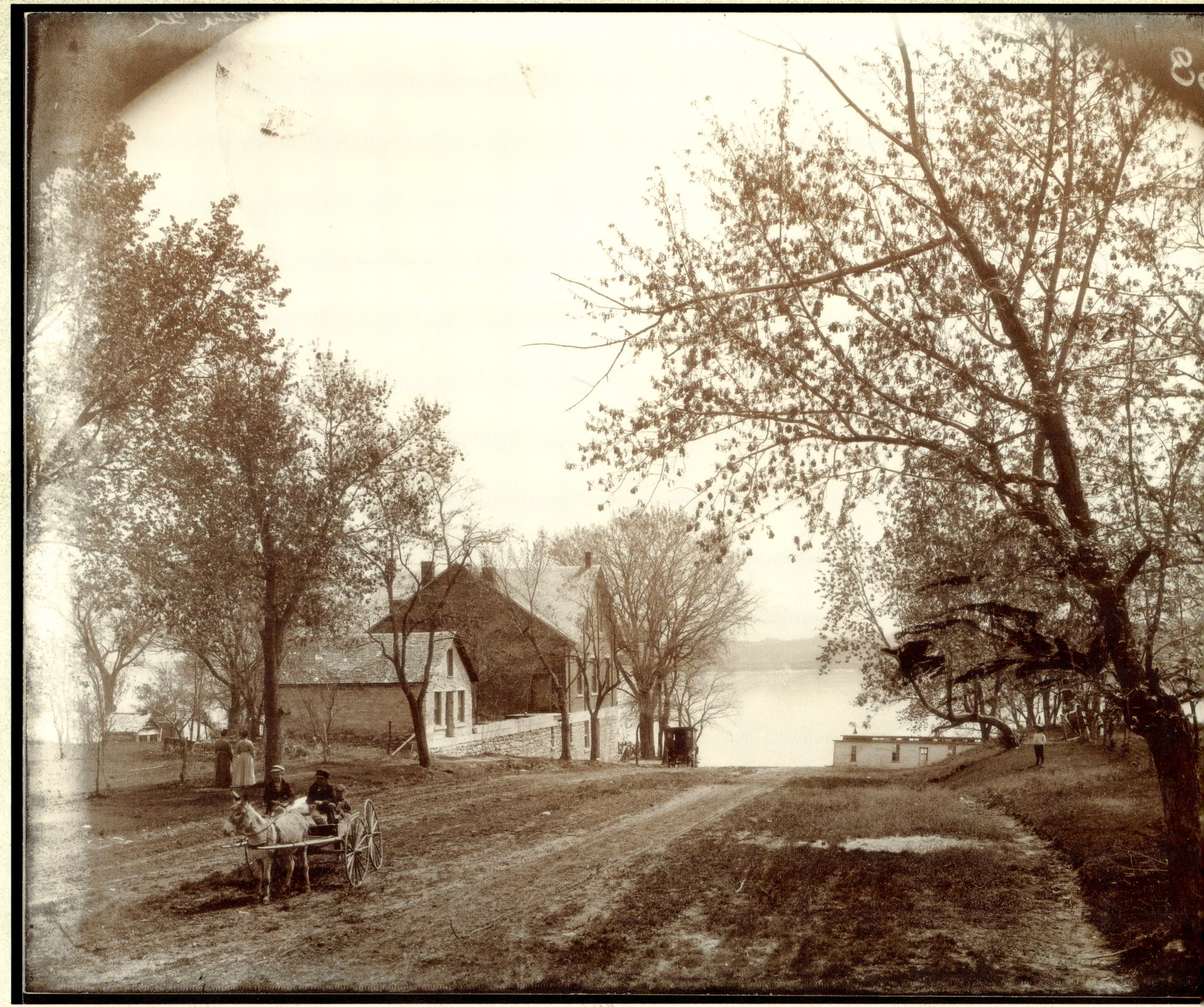

Riverside Mansion, site of the Nauvoo House, Nauvoo, Illinois, May 2, 1907, Anderson Collection, LDS Church History Library, Salt Lake City, Utah.

unique and important role in the restoration of these temple blessings in Nauvoo. Brigham Young, Heber C. Kimball, and Willard Richards were among the first persons to receive the endowment in May 1842.[18] Joseph Smith had increasingly come to rely upon the Twelve and asked Young to help him administer the ordinances. During this remarkable period of doctrinal revelation in Nauvoo, the Prophet began to prepare the Twelve, with Brigham at their head, to continue as leaders of the Church after his departure.[19] The Lord had tested these men's discipleship and proved that they were to be trusted to lead the Church after Joseph Smith died.

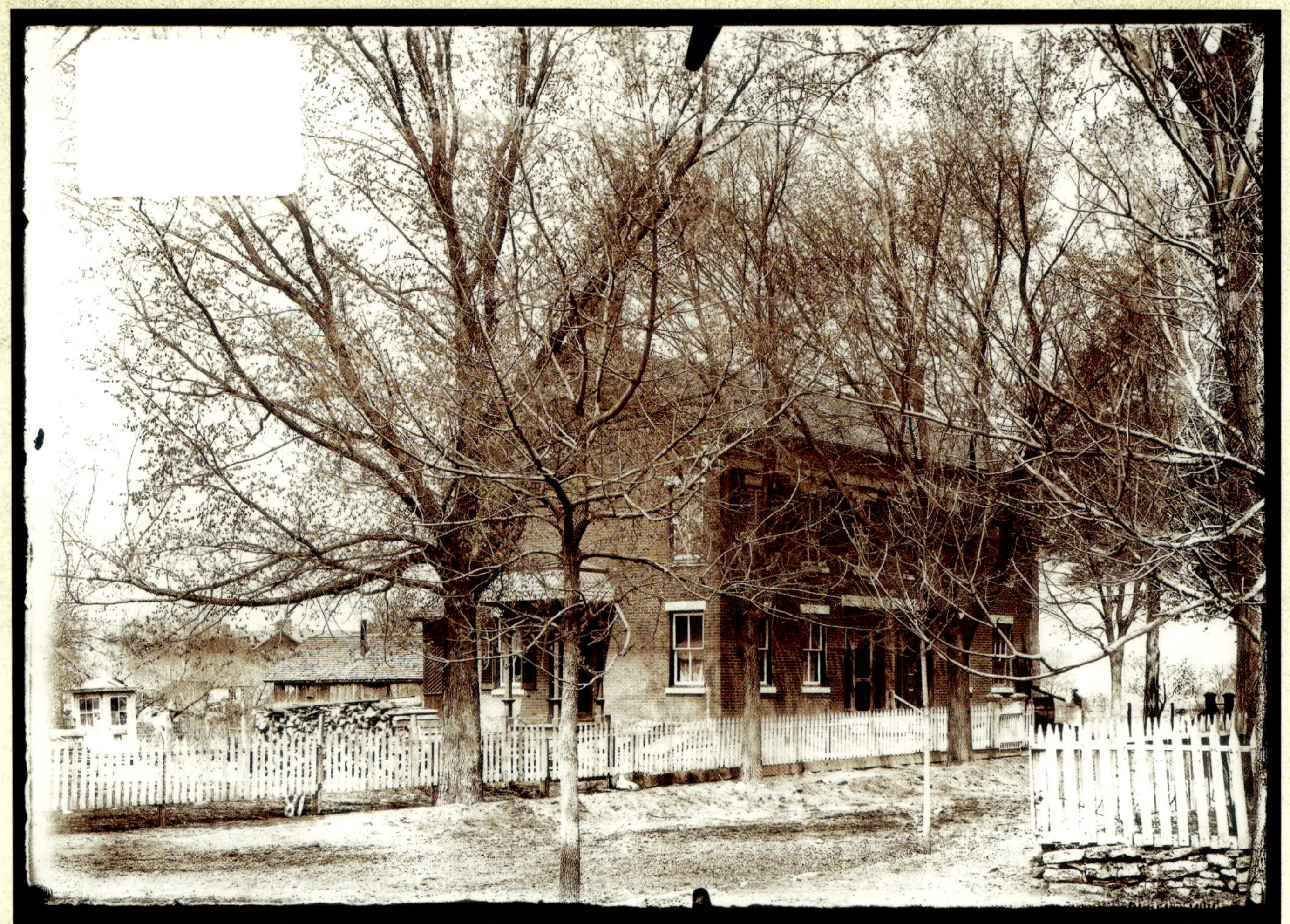

Erastus Snow-Nathaniel Ashby duplex, Nauvoo, Illinois, May 4, 1907, Anderson Collection, LDS Church History Library, Salt Lake City, Utah.

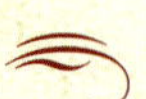

A principal test in Nauvoo was plural marriage.[20] A revelation on plural marriage was recorded for the first time on paper in Nauvoo, but the Prophet had taught and begun to practice it before then (D&C 132). The doctrine and the introduction of the practice tried the hearts and souls of both men and women in the Church.[21] By 1844 some of Joseph Smith's closest associates, including William Law of the First Presidency, had failed the test. Some of them left the Church, and others became bitter enemies of the Prophet and his supporters. There were moments of doubt and rebellion by many who eventually accepted Joseph Smith's prophetic role. It was a difficult, challenging time.

Interestingly, some men and women who ultimately rejected plural marriage continued to believe that Joseph Smith had been called of God but that he had become a fallen prophet. They cited doctrinal developments such as the introduction of plural marriage and temple sealings as evidence. With good humor the Prophet said in April 1844, "I had rather be a fallen true prophet, than a false prophet."[22] Nonetheless, Joseph testified that he was not a fallen prophet and that he was never "any nearer to God than at the present time."[23]

On Sunday, April 7, 1844, the Prophet delivered his last general conference address, often called the King Follett discourse.[24] The death of King Follett on March 9, 1844, nearly a month earlier, influenced its subject matter—the

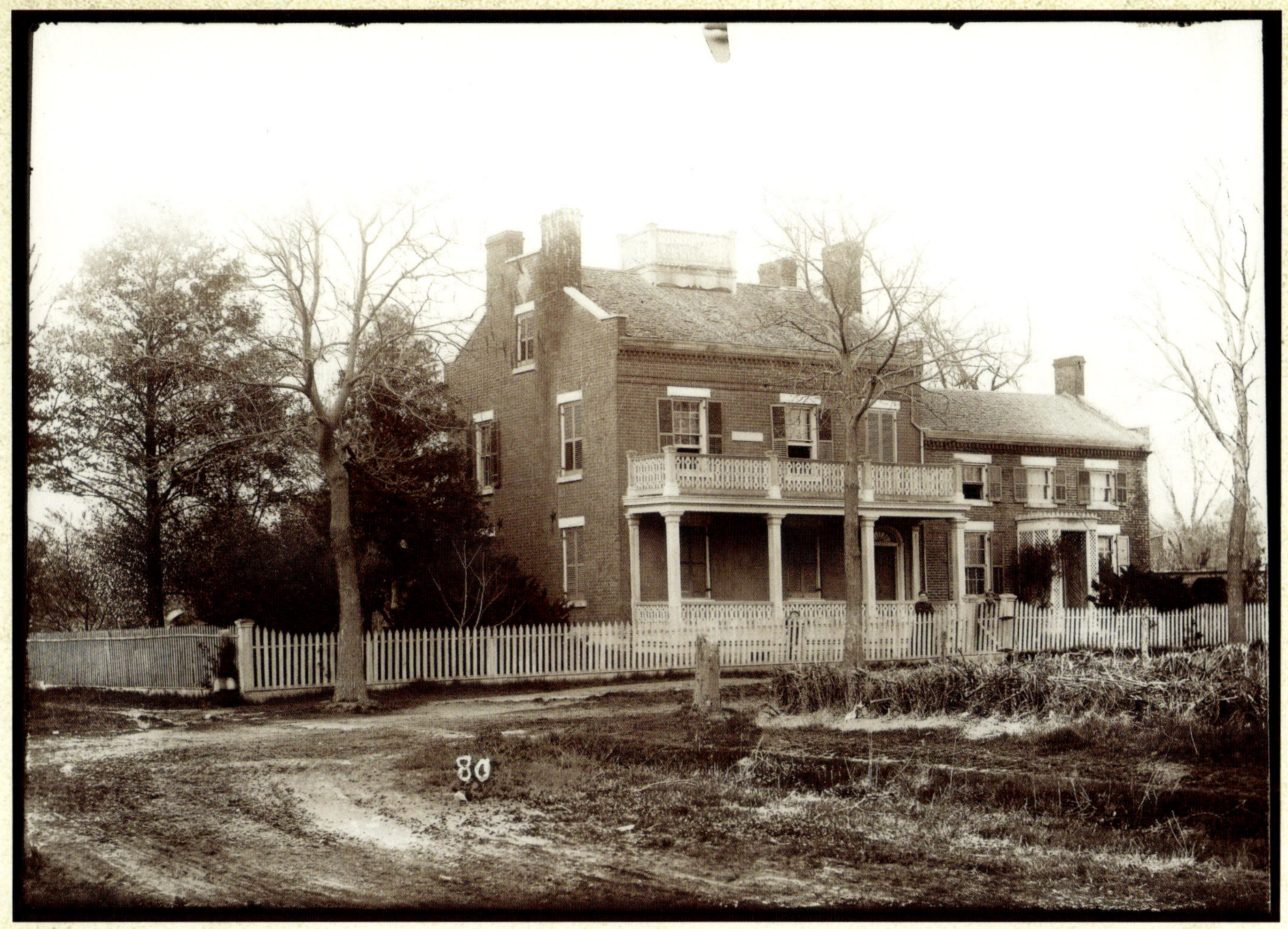

Home of Heber Chase and Vilate Murray Kimball, Nauvoo, Illinois, May 1907, Anderson Collection, LDS Church History Library, Salt Lake City, Utah.

eternity of man.[25] For William Law, a former member of the First Presidency, and some lay members, Joseph's teachings were simply too much. Law wrote in his diary: "Conference is over, and some of the most blasphemous doctrines have been taught by J. Smith and others ever heard of. . . . It was a strange conference, was not organized at all, and was managed in a most unprecedented manner."[26]

Law, along with three hundred to five hundred people, began to organize a reformed church in Nauvoo.[27] This break-off church reflected, in many ways, the 1830s Kirtland-period organization of the Church, setting aside the Nauvoo-period revelations, ordinances, and practices.

Most Saints in Nauvoo, however, including members of the Twelve, remained faithful and testified that Joseph remained "a true Prophet of God, ordained of God to lay the foundation of His Church and Kingdom in the last dispensation and fullness of times."[28] Their reaction to the Prophet's conference address was fundamentally different from the response of Law and other dissidents. For example, Wilford Woodruff recorded some of the discourse in his personal journal and opined, "3 o'clock P.M. April Sunday 7th 1844. The following important, edifying, and interesting discourse was delivered by President Joseph Smith."[29]

Joseph Fielding, who had been sent to the British Isles by Joseph Smith in 1837 in the midst of the Kirtland crisis, considered the conference a positive witness of the prophetic call of Joseph Smith. He wrote:

"As to me I have evidence enough that Joseph is not

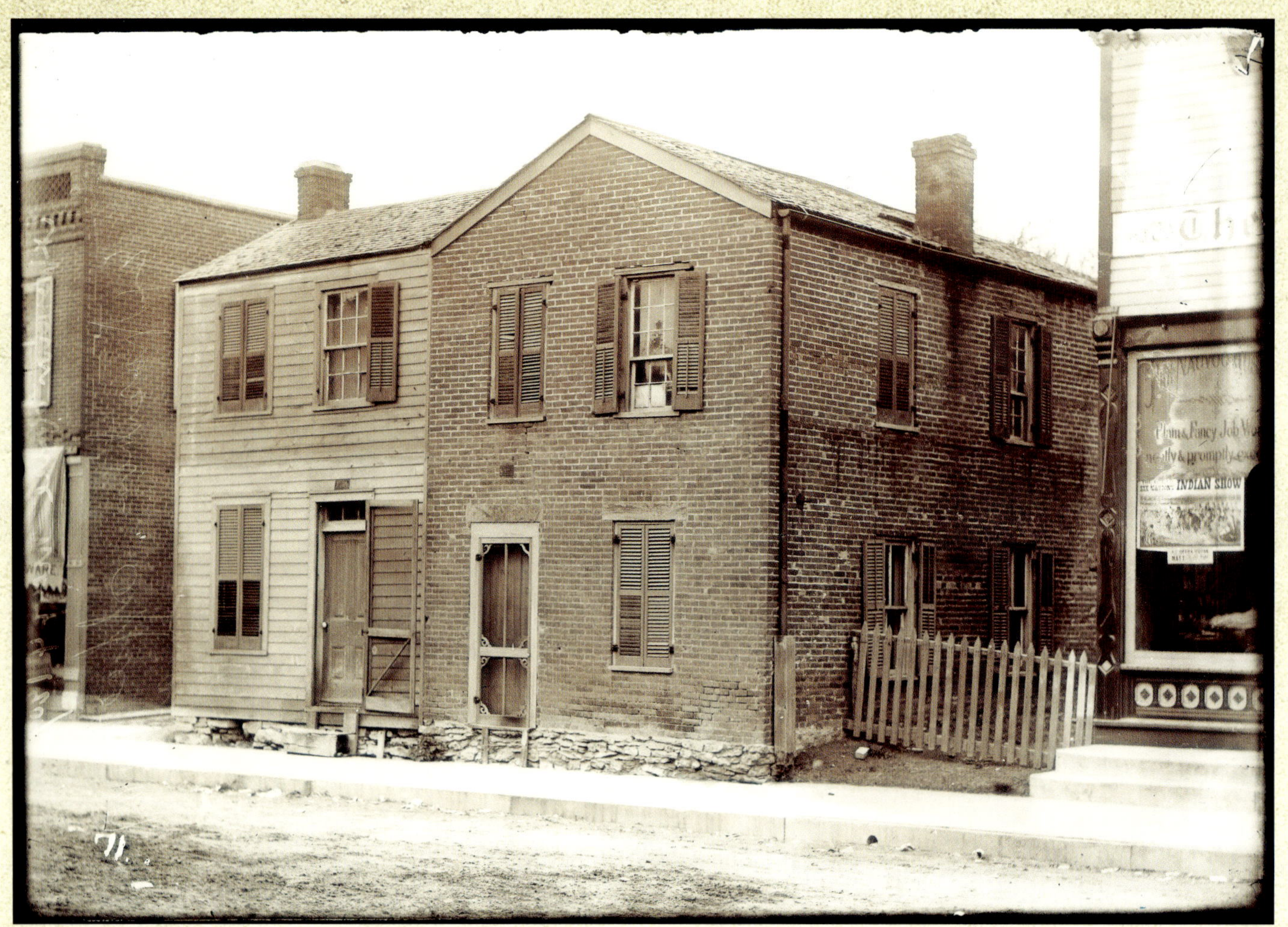

The Nauvoo Expositor *building, Nauvoo, Illinois, May 1907, Anderson Collection, L. Tom Perry Special Collections, Brigham Young University, Provo, Utah.*

fallen. . . . Our annual conference began and continued four days. Joseph's discourse on the origin of man, the nature of God, and the resurrection was the most interesting matter of this time, and any one that could not see in him the spirit of inspiration of God must be dark; they might have known that he was not a fallen Prophet even if they thought he was fallen."[30]

William Clayton, who had arrived in Nauvoo six weeks earlier, said of Joseph's Nauvoo sermons in his journal, "It seems like heaven began on earth *and the power of God is with us*."[31] To him, the doctrinal revelations of Nauvoo were not only prophetic but also exciting.

A few prominent dissidents published the first and only issue of the *Nauvoo Expositor* on June 7, 1844.

A few prominent dissidents published the first and only issue of the *Nauvoo Expositor* on June 7, 1844. Their purpose was to embarrass the Church, incite animosity from non-Mormons in the region, and rally support for the newly organized Reformed Church.[32] Apparently, Joseph Smith and other officials believed that the paper had the potential to incite violence against the Saints. Following a lengthy debate on what actions they should take in this situation, the city council, with Mayor Joseph Smith's approval, declared the paper a public nuisance.[33] According to one legal scholar, city officials acted within their legal jurisdiction to destroy the press on which the newspaper was printed.[34] Nevertheless, this act incited opposition and led to their arrest. This began a series of legal maneuvers that placed Joseph Smith in jail at the county seat in Carthage without sufficient protection.[35]

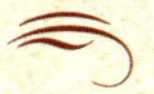

Before he surrendered himself to the legal authorities, the Prophet gave a sermon on the Godhead on June 16 in the grove east of the temple.[36] The sermon was an important doctrinal statement and a summary of his teachings of the Nauvoo period.

The conspiracy to place Joseph Smith in custody in Carthage culminated in the murder of the Prophet on Thursday, June 27 (D&C 135:1). The next day the bodies of Joseph and Hyrum Smith were returned to a shocked Nauvoo, where they were secretly buried.[37]

The succession crisis that followed the Prophet's death was not fully resolved for every Latter-day Saint, but most Church members remained loyal to Brigham Young and the Quorum of the Twelve Apostles and sustained them on August 8, 1844, as the rightful successors of Joseph Smith. The Twelve fulfilled the Prophet's vision and provided prophetic leadership to the Church through the Nauvoo period and beyond. Converts, especially from the British Isles, continued to flow to Nauvoo. Work on the temple and on homes and businesses increased. Eventually, the Prophet's enemies realized that killing him had not destroyed the Church. Opposition and physical violence rose again, forcing the Saints to depart their beautiful city and their beloved temple.

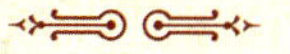

Brigham Young was concerned with those left behind in Nauvoo, even offering to sell the recently completed temple to help the poor get away from the city.

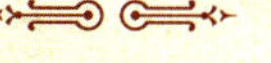

The first Latter-day Saints departed Nauvoo in February 1846. People continued to leave the city during the next few weeks and months. Most of those who left in the last group in September 1846 (around six hundred people) were sick or destitute. During his journey across Iowa in the spring of 1846, President Brigham Young was concerned with those left behind in Nauvoo, even offering to sell the recently completed temple to help the poor get away from the city.

Messengers going back and forth along the Mormon trail through Iowa delivered reports to Church leaders. In September the leaders learned about the Battle of Nauvoo, which forced the remaining Saints out of their homes to seek survival along a two-mile stretch of the west bank of the Mississippi River above Montrose, Iowa. During a Sunday meeting at the temporary Church headquarters at Winter Quarters, President Young asked the Saints to help their brothers and sisters: "Let the fire of the covenant which you made in the House of the Lord, burn in your hearts like flames unquenchable till you, by yourselves or delegates . . . [can] rise up with his team and go straightway and bring a load of the poor from Nauvoo . . . [for] this is a day of action and not of argument."[38] Church leaders recognized that the task was urgent because few of the refugees had food supplies or sufficient shelter to protect themselves from the elements. A rescue party had already been dispatched from the Missouri River Valley, but Brigham Young wanted more help—a second rescue mission. As preparation for the second

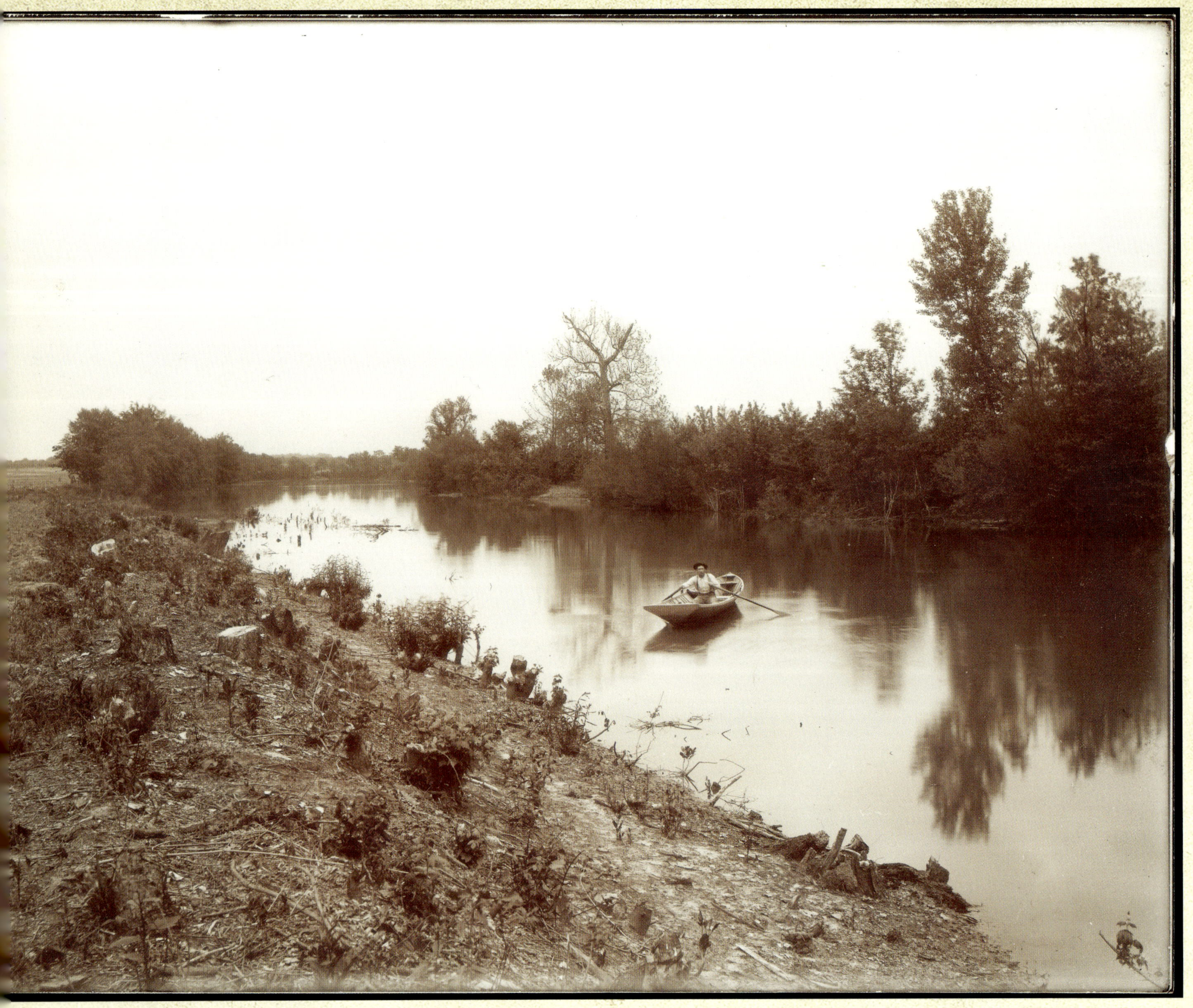

Potter's Slough, traditional site of the miracle of the quail in October 1846, near Montrose, Lee County, Iowa, May 29, 1907, Anderson Collection, LDS Church History Library, Salt Lake City, Utah.

group's departure was made, the first rescue party arrived at the Mississippi River on October 6 ready to help the suffering Saints.

A few days later, Thomas Bullock noted, a flock of quail flew around and into the camp: "The boys caught about 20 alive. . . . every man and woman and child had quails to eat for their dinner. After dinner the flock increased in size. Captain Allen ordered the brethren not to kill; . . . not a gun was afterwards fired and the quails flew round the camp, many alighted in it; . . . this was repeated more than half a dozen times."[39] The Saints considered this a providential gift from God, who was leading the modern Camp of Israel toward the promised land.

Though they had left the city of Nauvoo and the temple, the Saints who gathered in the Missouri River Valley in the winter of 1846–47 under the direction of Brigham Young took with them the spirit of Nauvoo—its doctrine, its ordinances, and its hopes and dreams.

Today, the light and glory revealed in Nauvoo through the Prophet Joseph Smith continues to illuminate every home, meetinghouse, missionary training center, seminary and institute building, Church school campus, and temple throughout the world where the gospel is preached.

Today, the light and glory revealed in Nauvoo through the Prophet Joseph Smith continues to illuminate every home, meetinghouse, missionary training center, seminary and institute building, Church school campus, and temple throughout the world.

Epilogue

Profound Effects of the Restoration

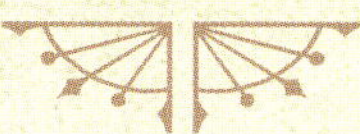

The ultimate effect of the Restoration may never be known on this side of the veil; however, some contributions are readily recognizable. Donald Q. Cannon, Larry E. Dahl, and John W. Welch, three colleagues at Brigham Young University, discussed in a two-part series in the *Ensign* several major doctrinal contributions that have come through the Restoration. They wrote:

"Although the Prophet Joseph Smith's mortal ministry was relatively brief—little more than fifteen years—his accomplishments and influence are eternal. Not only did he restore both the gospel and the church of Jesus Christ, as directed by the Lord, he also introduced, through the revelations he received and through his teachings, most of the major doctrines, practices, and ordinances that characterize The Church of Jesus Christ of Latter-day Saints."[1]

Their discussion centered on six specific teachings: "the nature of God and the Godhead, man's nature and his premortal existence, . . . the Creation, . . . the priesthood of God, scripture, and temples and their ordinances."[2] These six eternally significant topics are, in fact, interconnected.

Every individual who joined the Church in the 1830s, including Joseph Smith himself, was a convert.

Adding to these doctrinal insights, our colleague J. Spencer Fluhman has made an astute observation worth considering. He noted that every individual who joined the Church in the 1830s, including Joseph Smith himself, was a convert. Something happened that profoundly affected their lives and the lives of their descendants. Fluhman said, "What lingering Protestant attachments the early Saints might have held were systemically undone by the revelations."[3] This is a significant point. The restored gospel of Jesus Christ made Baptists, Catholics, Congregationalists, Jews, Methodists, and Presbyterians into Latter-day Saints.

A similar conversion occurred millennia earlier when the gospel of Jesus Christ made first-century Jews into Christians (remember that Peter, James, John, and Mary were all Jews). Though they continued to share the same scripture (the Old Testament) with their Jewish brothers and sisters, and they prayed, fasted, and sang hymns in ways that they had done before, the Savior's disciples had a new perspective as they read the scriptures and viewed life through the life and teachings of Jesus of Nazareth. Likewise, the early members of the restored Church of Jesus Christ—while continuing to share a common scripture (the Bible) and while praying, fasting, and singing many of the same hymns as other Christians—obtained a new perspective as they read the scriptures and experienced life through inspired translations (the Book of Mormon, the book of Abraham, and the Joseph Smith Translation of the Bible) and commandments and revelations (the Doctrine and Covenants) that came through the Prophet Joseph Smith, who was "blessed to open the last dispensation."[4]

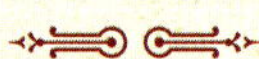

Today the message continues to spread as prophesied so many years ago.

Today the message continues to spread as prophesied: "The Standard of Truth has been erected; no unhallowed hand can stop the work from progressing; persecutions may rage, mobs may combine, armies may assemble, calumny may defame, but the truth of God will go forth boldly, nobly, and independent, till it has penetrated every continent, visited every clime, swept every country, and sounded in every ear, till the purposes of God shall be accomplished, and the Great Jehovah shall say the work is done."[5]

Notes

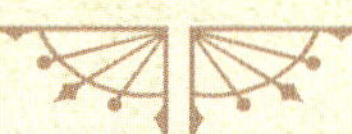

Prologue

1. Junius F. Wells to Joseph Fielding Smith, October 16, 1928, Church History Library, Salt Lake City.
2. Anderson, Diary, August 16, 1907, as cited in Holzapfel, Cottle, and Stoddard, *Church History in Black and White,* 4.
3. Anderson, Diary, August 14, 1907, as cited in Holzapfel, Cottle, and Stoddard, *Church History in Black and White,* 4.
4. Anderson, Diary, August 17, 1907, as cited in Holzapfel, Cottle, and Stoddard, *Church History in Black and White,* 4.

Introduction
Glass Plates and Pen, Paper, and Ink

1. This material will eventually be published in *The Joseph Smith Papers,* a series projected to comprise more than a dozen volumes. General editors Dean C. Jessee, Ronald K. Esplin, and Richard Lyman Bushman have noted, "The goal of the Joseph Smith Papers Project is to present every extant document written by Smith or by his scribes in his behalf, as well as other records that were created under his direction or that reflect his personal instruction or involvement" (Jessee, Ashurst-McGee, and Jensen, eds., *Journals,* 1:lix).
2. Joseph Smith to William Phelps, November 27, 1832, Joseph Smith Collection, Church History Library, Salt Lake City.
3. Jessee, "Priceless Words and Fallible Memories," 23.
4. Kirtland Council Minute Book, February 27, 1835, Church History Library, Salt Lake City, 85; or Smith, *History of the Church,* 2:198–99.
5. See Jessee, "The Writing of Joseph Smith's History," 439–72.
6. See Wadsworth, *Through Camera Eyes.*

1
George Edward Anderson's Photography by John Telford

1. Savage, Diary, 1894.
2. Anderson, Diary, June 8, 1907, as cited in Holzapfel, Cottle, and Stoddard, *Church History in Black and White,* 116.

2
New England

1. Smith, *History of the Church,* 6:89.
2. The "gore" was originally a "strip of unsurveyed land ¾ mile wide" stretching between Tunbridge and Royalton Townships. The result of a surveying error, the "gore" was annexed to Tunbridge Township in 1785 (Hartley and Anderson, *New England and Eastern Canada,* 112–13).
3. Smith, *Biographical Sketches,* 31.
4. See Anderson, *Lucy's Book,* 168.
5. Smith, *Biographical Sketches,* 54.
6. See Hartley and Anderson, *New England and Eastern Canada,* 51.
7. Smith, *Biographical Sketches,* 56.
8. Smith, *Biographical Sketches,* 66.
9. Anderson, *Lucy's Book,* 169.
10. Smith, *Biographical Sketches,* 66.
11. Evans, "Blast from the Past," 52–57.
12. Evans, "Blast from the Past," 52–57.

3
New York and Pennsylvania

1. Smith, *Biographical Sketches,* 71.
2. See Smith, *Personal Writings,* ed. Jessee, 11.
3. Hinckley, "What Are People Asking about Us?" 71.
4. See Pratt, *Autobiography,* 31.

5. Smith, "Old Soldier's Testimony," 643.
6. Oliver Cowdery to "Dear Brother," in Smith, *Papers of Joseph Smith,* ed. Jessee, 1:81–82.
7. Oliver Cowdery to W. W. Phelps, in Smith, *Papers of Joseph Smith,* ed. Jessee, 1:78–79.
8. Smith, *Biographical Sketches,* 105.
9. Hedges, "'All My Endeavors to Preserve Them,'" 22.
10. Hedges, "'All My Endeavors to Preserve Them,'" 22–23; spelling and punctuation modernized.
11. Smith, *Personal Writings,* ed. Jessee, 13; spelling and punctuation modernized.
12. Smith, *Papers of Joseph Smith,* ed. Jessee, 1:287.
13. See Smith, *Biographical Sketches,* 126; see also Hedges, "'All My Endeavors to Preserve Them.'"
14. Smith, *Personal Writings,* ed. Jessee, 14; Smith, *Biographical Sketches,* 124; see also Hedges, "'All My Endeavors to Preserve Them.'"
15. Smith, *Biographical Sketches,* 124, 131.
16. Smith, *Biographical Sketches,* 129.
17. Oliver Cowdery, in Smith, *Papers of Joseph Smith,* ed. Jessee, 1:29; spelling and punctuation modernized.
18. Smith, *Papers of Joseph Smith,* ed. Jessee, 1:293.
19. Smith, *Papers of Joseph Smith,* ed. Jessee, 1:292.
20. Addison Everett to Joseph F. Smith, January 16, 1882, St. George, Utah, as cited in Cannon, "Priesthood Restoration Documents," 199n11; spelling and punctuation modernized.
21. Smith, *Biographical Sketches,* 135.
22. See Smith, *Papers of Joseph Smith,* ed. Jessee, 1:293.
23. See Anderson, *Lucy's Book,* 450.
24. Smith, *Papers of Joseph Smith,* ed. Jessee, 1:293, 294.
25. Smith, *Papers of Joseph Smith,* ed. Jessee, 1:294.
26. Smith, *Papers of Joseph Smith,* ed. Jessee, 1:299.
27. Smith, *Papers of Joseph Smith,* ed. Jessee, 1:295–96.
28. Smith, *Papers of Joseph Smith,* ed. Jessee, 1:297.
29. Smith, *Biographical Sketches,* 139.
30. Smith, *Biographical Sketches,* 139.
31. See Smith, *Biographical Sketches,* 143–46.
32. Hedges, "The Refractory Abner Cole," 447–49.
33. "An Act to Provide for the Incorporation of Religious Societies," section III, 1813, as cited in Porter, *Study of the Origins,* 157.
34. Smith, *Papers of Joseph Smith,* ed. Jessee, 1:303.
35. See Smith, *Papers of Joseph Smith,* ed. Jessee, 1:304.
36. Smith, *Papers of Joseph Smith,* ed. Jessee, 1:305–6.
37. Smith, *Papers of Joseph Smith,* ed. Jessee, 1:319.
38. Smith, *Papers of Joseph Smith,* ed. Jessee, 1:321.
39. Smith, *Papers of Joseph Smith,* ed. Jessee, 1:323.

4
Ohio

1. Anderson, Diary, August 6, 1907, as cited in Holzapfel, Cottle, and Stoddard, *Church History in Black and White,* 143.
2. See Holzapfel, *Exodus Story,* 61–72.
3. See Jessee, Ashurst-McGee, and Jensen, eds., *Journals,* 1:xxii–xxv.
4. The Prophet received additional revelations in New York and Missouri during 1831, making this a remarkable revelatory year for Joseph Smith (see Underwood, "Flood of Revelations," 77–100).
5. This manuscript book is reproduced in Jensen, Woodford, and Harper, eds., *Revelations and Translations,* Vol. 1.
6. A brief description of the various appearances of the Father and the Son in Ohio is found in Anderson, *Joseph Smith's Kirtland,* 107–13.
7. Bushman, *Rough Stone Rolling,* 195–96.
8. The office of bishop was established in 1831, the same year that high priests were called and ordained; the office of patriarch was established two years later, in 1833. The First Presidency was formed in 1832, stake presidencies and high councils in 1834, and the quorums of the Twelve Apostles and the seventy in 1835.
9. Bushman, *Rough Stone Rolling,* 153; see also Bushman, *Mormonism,* 49–63.
10. Caroline Crosby Memoirs, Church History Library, Salt Lake City.
11. Joseph Smith to William W. Phelps, January 11, 1833, Joseph Smith Collection, Church History Library, Salt Lake City.
12. Joseph Smith, Discourse, Kirtland, Ohio, November 12, 1835, Joseph Smith Journal, as cited in Smith, *Papers of Joseph Smith,* ed. Jessee, 2:76–77; spelling and punctuation modernized.
13. W. W. Phelps, as cited in Harper, "'Pentecost and Endowment Indeed,'" 331.
14. Oliver Cowdery Sketch Book, January 16, 1836, Church History Library, Salt Lake City.
15. Jessee, Ashurst-McGee, and Jensen, eds., *Journals,* 1:166–67.
16. Oliver Cowdery, as cited in Harper, "'Pentecost and Endowment Indeed,'" 338, 344.
17. The full account of the vision is preserved in Joseph Smith Journal, Joseph Smith Collection, Church History Library, Salt Lake City, as cited in Jessee, Ashurst-McGee, and Jensen, eds., *Journals,* 1:166–68.
18. See Oliver Cowdery Sketch Book, March 26, 1836, Church History Library, Salt Lake City.
19. Joseph Smith Journal, March 30, 1836, Joseph Smith Collection, Church History Library, Salt Lake City, as cited in Jessee, Ashurst-McGee, and Jensen, eds., *Journals,* 1:216.
20. Smith, *Papers of Joseph Smith,* ed. Jessee, 2:209.
21. Esplin, "Kirtland Crisis," 261.

22. Esplin, "Kirtland Crisis," 261.
23. Esplin, "Kirtland Crisis," 262–63.
24. Esplin, "Kirtland Crisis," 263.
25. A comprehensive study of this mission is found in Allen, Esplin, and Whittaker, *Men with a Mission,* 20–53.
26. Smith, *History of the Church,* 2:489.
27. Joseph Smith Journal, Joseph Smith Collection, Church History Library, Salt Lake City, as cited in Jessee, Ashurst-McGee, and Jensen, eds., *Journals,* 1:283–84.

5
Missouri

1. Smith, *Papers of Joseph Smith,* ed. Jessee, 1:358, 360.
2. See Holzapfel and Cottle, *Old Mormon Kirtland and Missouri,* 196.
3. Holzapfel and Cottle, *Old Mormon Kirtland and Missouri,* 186.
4. Smith, *History of the Church,* 1:358.
5. Smith, *History of the Church,* 1:358.
6. See Romig, "Temple Lot Discoveries and the RLDS Temple," 321, 323–24.
7. See Holzapfel and Cottle, *Old Mormon Kirtland and Missouri,* 196.
8. Smith, *History of the Church,* 1:359.
9. Phelps, "To His Excellency, Daniel Dunklin, Governor of the State of Missouri," 114.
10. See Smith, *History of the Church,* 1:398–99.
11. Smith, *History of the Church,* 1:336–37.
12. Smith, *Papers of Joseph Smith,* ed. Jessee, 2:244; spelling and punctuation modernized.
13. Albert Rockwood, as cited in Holzapfel and Cottle, *Old Mormon Kirtland and Missouri,* 234.
14. See Baugh, "The Battle between Mormon and Missouri Militia," 87–91.
15. Pratt, *Autobiography,* 154.
16. See Baugh, "The Battle between Mormon and Missouri Militia," 91–92.
17. Pratt, *Autobiography,* 154.
18. See Baugh, "The Battle between Mormon and Missouri Militia," 92–93, 95.
19. See Baugh, "The Battle between Mormon and Missouri Militia," 93, 95–96.
20. See Baugh, "The Haun's Mill Massacre and the Extermination Order," 1–4.
21. Smith, *History of the Church,* 3:184.
22. See Benson, "Haun's Mill Massacre," 109.
23. See Benson, "Haun's Mill Massacre," 109.
24. Smith, *History of the Church,* 3:185.
25. Angus Cannon, as cited in Anderson, *Investigating the Book of Mormon Witnesses,* 90.

6
Illinois

1. See Anderson, Diary, May 1, 1907, as cited in Holzapfel, Cottle, and Stoddard, *Church History in Black and White,* 41. Anderson returned to Missouri to photograph more sites there before returning to Nauvoo on May 29, 1907. He continued his photographic work in Nauvoo until June 3, 1907 (Holzapfel, Cottle, and Stoddard, *Church History in Black and White,* 106–13).
2. Anderson, Diary, May 2, 1907, as cited in Holzapfel, Cottle, and Stoddard, *Church History in Black and White,* 41.
3. Madsen, *In Their Own Words,* 4.
4. Although we have a record of only about 10 percent of Joseph Smith's discourses, the sermons of the Nauvoo period, particularly the last eighteen months of his life, are fairly well documented. Approximately thirty-five talks were recorded during the closing months of his ministry (see Jessee, "Priceless Words and Fallible Memories," 23).
5. Nancy Tracey Autobiography, Utah State Historical Society, Salt Lake City.
6. Clark, *Messages of the First Presidency,* 3:134.
7. Harper, *Making Sense of the Doctrine and Covenants,* 460.
8. Rushton, "Proclamations," 954–55.
9. See Black, "Nauvoo House," 825–26.
10. See Cowan, "Nauvoo Temple," 828–30.
11. See Leonard, *Nauvoo,* 242–65.
12. Joseph Smith Journal, May 1, 1842, Joseph Smith Collection, Church History Library, Salt Lake City, as cited in Smith, *Papers of Joseph Smith,* ed. Jessee, 2:379.
13. Smith, *History of the Church,* 4:602.
14. Smith, *History of the Church,* 4:604–5.
15. Smith, *History of the Church,* 4:604.
16. Smith, *History of the Church,* 5:2.
17. Relief Society Minutes, May 27, 1842, Church History Library, Salt Lake City.
18. See Smith, *Papers of Joseph Smith,* ed. Jessee, 2:380.
19. See Jorgensen, "Mantle of the Prophet Joseph," 343–480.
20. See Leonard, *Nauvoo,* 343–56.
21. See Holzapfel and Holzapfel, *Women of Nauvoo,* 86–103.
22. Ehat and Cook, eds., *Words of Joseph,* 367.
23. Smith, *History of the Church,* 6:287–88; see also Ehat and Cook, eds., *Words of Joseph Smith,* 340.
24. See Bushman, *Rough Stone Rolling,* 533–37; Cannon and Perkins, *Ohio and Illinois,* 174–76.
25. See Smith, *History of the Church,* 6:302–17 and Smith, *Teachings,* 342–62. For transcriptions of the original notes, see Ehat and Cook, eds., *Words of Joseph Smith,* 340–62.

26. William Law, Diary, April 15, 1844, in private possession; spelling and punctuation modernized.
27. See Cook, *William Law,* 54n41.
28. Wilford Woodruff, Statement, March 19, 1897, Church History Library, Salt Lake City, as cited in Holzapfel and Harper, "'This Is My Testimony,'" 112–16.
29. Wilford Woodruff, Journal, April 7, 1844, Church History Library, Salt Lake City, as cited in Kenney, *Wilford Woodruff's Journal,* 2:382; spelling, capitalization, and punctuation modernized.
30. Joseph Fielding, Diary, April 1844, Church History Library, Salt Lake City, as cited in Ehat, "They Might Have Known That He Was Not a Fallen Prophet," 147–48; spelling and punctuation modernized.
31. William Clayton, Diary, April 18, 1844, Church History Library, Salt Lake City, as cited in Ehat, "'It Seems Like Heaven Began on Earth,'" 266.
32. See Smith, *History of the Church,* 6:430; see also Cannon and Perkins, *Ohio and Illinois,* 185–86.
33. See Smith, *History of the Church,* 6:445.
34. See Oaks, "Joseph Smith in a Personal World," 160–61; Oaks, "Suppression of the *Nauvoo Expositor,*" 862–903.
35. For more on the legal details of the Prophet's martyrdom and the subsequent trials of his murderers, see Oaks and Hill, *Carthage Conspiracy.*
36. See Ehat and Cook, eds., *Words of Joseph Smith,* 378–82; see also Cannon and Perkins, *Ohio and Illinois,* 174–76.
37. See Smith, *History of the Church,* 6:627–29; see also Cannon and Perkins, *Ohio and Illinois,* 139–40.
38. Journal History of the Church, September 26, 1846.
39. Thomas Bullock, Journal, October 9, 1846, Church History Library, Salt Lake City.

Epilogue
Profound Effects of the Restoration

1. Cannon, Dahl, and Welch, "Restoration of Major Doctrines," 27.
2. Cannon, Dahl, and Welch, "Restoration of Major Doctrines," 28.
3. Fluhman, "Authority, Power, and the 'Government of the Church of Christ,'" 216.
4. William W. Phelps, "Praise to the Man," *Hymns,* no. 27.
5. Smith, *History of the Church,* 4:540.

Sources

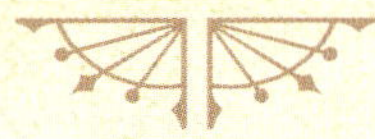

Allen, James B., Ronald K. Esplin, and David J. Whittaker. *Men with a Mission: The Quorum of the Twelve Apostles in the British Isles, 1837–1841.* Salt Lake City: Deseret Book, 1991.

Anderson, A. Gary, Donald Q. Cannon, Larry E. Dahl, and Larry C. Porter. *New England and Eastern Canada.* Vol. 1 of *Sacred Places: A Comprehensive Guide to Early LDS Historical Sites.* Edited by LaMar C. Berrett. Salt Lake City: Bookcraft, 1999.

Anderson, George Edward. Diary, Manuscript Collection, 1901–28. Archives. The Church of Jesus Christ of Latter-day Saints, Salt Lake City.

Anderson, Karl Ricks. *Joseph Smith's Kirtland: Eyewitness Accounts.* Salt Lake City: Deseret Book, 1989.

Anderson, Lavina Fielding, ed. *Lucy's Book: A Critical Edition of Lucy Mack Smith's Family Memoir.* Salt Lake City: Signature Books, 2001.

Anderson, Richard L. *Investigating the Book of Mormon Witnesses.* Salt Lake City: Deseret Book, 1981.

Baugh, Alexander L. "The Battle between Mormon and Missouri Militia at Crooked River." In Garr and Johnson, eds., *Missouri,* 85–103.

———. "The Haun's Mill Massacre and the Extermination Order of Missouri Governor Lilburn W. Boggs." *Religious Studies Center Newsletter,* September 1997, 1–5.

Benson, Alvin K. "The Haun's Mill Massacre: Some Examples of Tragedy and Superior Faith." In Garr and Johnson, eds., *Missouri,* 105–18.

Bullock, Thomas. Journal, October 9, 1846. Church History Library, Salt Lake City.

Bushman, Richard Lyman. *Joseph Smith: Rough Stone Rolling.* New York: Alfred Knopf, 2005.

———. *Mormonism: A Very Short Introduction.* New York: Oxford University Press, 2008.

Cannon, Brian Q., and others. "Priesthood Restoration Documents." *BYU Studies* 35, no. 4 (1995–96): 162–207.

Cannon, Donald Q., and Keith W. Perkins. *Ohio and Illinois.* Vol. 3 of *Sacred Places: A Comprehensive Guide to Early LDS Historical Sites.* Edited by LaMar C. Berrett. Salt Lake City: Deseret Book, 2001.

Cannon, Donald Q., Larry E. Dahl, and John W. Welch. "The Restoration of Major Doctrines through Joseph Smith: The Godhead, Mankind, and the Creation." *Ensign,* January 1989, 26–33.

———. "The Restoration of Major Doctrines through Joseph Smith: Priesthood, the Word of God, and the Temple." *Ensign,* February 1989, 7–13.

Clark, James R., comp. *Messages of the First Presidency of The Church of Jesus Christ of Latter-day Saints.* 6 vols. Salt Lake City: Bookcraft, 1965–71.

Cook, Lyndon W. *William Law.* Orem, Utah: Grandin, 1994.

Cowdery, Oliver. Sketch Book, January 16, 1836, and March 26, 1836. Church History Library, Salt Lake City.

Crosby, Caroline. Memoirs. Church History Library, Salt Lake City.

Ehat, Andrew F. "'It Seems Like Heaven Began on Earth': Joseph Smith and the Constitution of the Kingdom of God." *BYU Studies* 20, no. 3 (Spring 1980): 253–80.

———. "'They Might Have Known That He Was Not a Fallen Prophet'—The Nauvoo Journal of Joseph Fielding." *BYU Studies* 19, no. 2 (Winter 1979): 133–66.

Ehat, Andrew F., and Lyndon W. Cook, eds. *The Words of Joseph*

Smith. Provo, Utah: Religious Studies Center, Brigham Young University, 1980.

Esplin, Ronald K. "Joseph Smith and the Kirtland Crisis, 1837." In Holzapfel and Jackson, *Joseph Smith, the Prophet and Seer,* 261–90.

Evans, Robert. "Blast from the Past." *Smithsonian* 33, no. 4 (July 2002): 52–57.

Faulring, Scott H., ed. *An American Prophet's Record: The Diaries and Journals of Joseph* Smith. Salt Lake City: Signature Books, 1989.

Fluhman, J. Spencer. "Authority, Power, and the 'Government of the Church of Christ,' 1835." In Holzapfel and Jackson, *Joseph Smith, the Prophet and Seer,* 195–232.

Francis, Rell G. *The Utah Photographs of George Edward Anderson.* Lincoln, Neb.: University of Nebraska Press, 1979.

Garr, Arnold H., Donald Q. Cannon, and Richard O. Cowan, eds. *Encyclopedia of Latter-day Saint History.* Salt Lake City: Deseret Book, 2000.

Garr, Arnold K., and Clark V. Johnson, eds. *Missouri,* a vol. in *Regional Studies in Latter-day Saint History.* Provo, Utah: Department of Church History and Doctrine, Brigham Young University, 1994.

Harper, Steven C. *Making Sense of the Doctrine and Covenants: A Guided Tour through the Revelations.* Salt Lake City: Deseret Book, 2008.

Hartley, William G., and A. Gary Anderson. *Iowa and Nebraska.* Vol. 5 of *Sacred Places: A Comprehensive Guide to Early LDS Historical Sites.* Edited by LaMar C. Berrett. Salt Lake City: Deseret Book, 2006.

Hedges, Andrew H. "'All My Endeavors to Preserve Them': Protecting the Plates in Palmyra, 22 September–December 1827." *Journal of Book of Mormon Studies* 8, no. 2 (1999): 14–23.

———. "The Refractory Abner Cole." In *Revelation, Reason, and Faith: Essays in Honor of Truman G. Madsen,* edited by Donald W. Parry, Daniel C. Peterson, and Stephen D. Ricks, 447–75. Provo, Utah: FARMS, 2002.

Hinckley, Gordon B. Hinckley. "What Are People Asking about Us?" *Ensign,* November 1998, 70–72.

Holzapfel, Richard Neitzel. *The Exodus Story: Ancient and Modern Parallels.* Salt Lake City: Bookcraft, 1997.

Holzapfel, Richard Neitzel, and T. Jeffery Cottle. *Old Mormon Kirtland and Missouri: Historic Photographs and Guide.* Santa Ana, Calif.: Fieldbrook Productions, 1991.

Holzapfel, Richard Neitzel, T. Jeffery Cottle, and Ted D. Stoddard, eds. *Church History in Black and White: George Edward Anderson's Photographic Mission to Latter-day Saint Historical Sites.* Provo, Utah: Religious Studies Center, Brigham Young University, 1995.

Holzapfel, Richard Neitzel, and Steven C. Harper. "'This Is My Testimony, Spoken by Myself into a Talking Machine': Wilford Woodruff's 1897 Statement in Stereo." *BYU Studies* 45, no. 2 (Spring 2006): 112–16.

Holzapfel, Richard Neitzel, and Jeni Broberg Holzapfel. *Women of Nauvoo.* Salt Lake City: Bookcraft, 1992.

Holzapfel, Richard Neitzel, and Kent S. Jackson, eds. *Joseph Smith, the Prophet and Seer.* Provo, Utah: Religious Studies Center, Brigham Young University; Salt Lake City: Deseret Book, 2010.

Hymns of The Church of Jesus Christ of Latter-day Saints. Salt Lake City: The Church of Jesus Christ of Latter-day Saints, 1985.

Jensen, Robin Scott, Robert J. Woodford, and Steven C. Harper, eds. *Revelations and Translations, Volume 1: Manuscript Revelation Books.* Vol. 1 of the Revelations and Translations series of *The Joseph Smith Papers,* edited by Dean C. Jessee, Ronald K. Esplin, and Richard Lyman Bushman. Facsimile edition. Salt Lake City: Church Historian's Press, 2009.

Jessee, Dean C. "Priceless Words and Fallible Memories: Joseph Smith as Seen in the Effort to Preserve His Discourses." *BYU Studies* 31, no. 2 (Spring 1991): 19–40.

———. "The Writing of Joseph Smith's History." *BYU Studies* 11, no. 4 (Summer 1974): 439–72.

Jessee, Dean C., Mark Ashurst-McGee, and Richard L. Jensen, eds. *Journals, Volume 1: 1832–1839.* Vol. 1 of the Journals series of *The Joseph Smith Papers,* edited by Dean C. Jessee, Ronald K. Esplin, and Richard Lyman Bushman. Salt Lake City: Church Historian's Press, 2008.

Journal History of The Church of Jesus Christ of Latter-day Saints, September 26, 1846. Church History Library, Salt Lake City.

Kenney, Scott G., ed. *Wilford Woodruff's Journal, 1833–1898, Typescript.* 9 vols. Midvale, Utah: Signature Books, 1983–85

Kirtland Council Minute Book, February 27, 1835. Church History Library, Salt Lake City.

Law, William. Diary, April 15, 1844. In private possession.

Leonard, Glen M. *Nauvoo: A Place of Peace, a People of Promise.* Salt Lake City: Deseret Book, 2002.

Madsen, Carol Cornwall. *In Their Own Words: Women and the Story of Nauvoo.* Salt Lake City: Deseret Book, 1994.

Oaks, Dallin H. "The Suppression of the *Nauvoo Expositor.*" *Utah Law Review* 9 (1965): 862–903.

———. "Joseph Smith in a Personal World." In *The Worlds of Joseph*

Smith: A Bicentennial Conference at the Library of Congress, edited by John W. Welch, 153–72. Provo, Utah: Brigham Young University Press, 2006.

Oaks, Dallin H., and Marvin S. Hill. *Carthage Conspiracy: The Trial of the Accused Assassins of Joseph Smith.* Chicago: University of Illinois Press, 1975.

Phelps, W. W. "To His Excellency, Daniel Dunklin, Governor of the State of Missouri." *The Evening and the Morning Star,* December 1833, 114–15.

Porter, Larry C. *A Study of the Origins of The Church of Jesus Christ of Latter-day Saints in the States of New York and Pennsylvania.* Provo, Utah: Joseph Fielding Smith Institute for Latter-day Saint History and BYU Studies, 2000.

Pratt, Parley P. *Autobiography of Parley P. Pratt.* Salt Lake City: Deseret Book, 1985.

Relief Society Minutes, May 27, 1842. Church History Library, Salt Lake City.

Romig, Ronald E. "Temple Lot Discoveries and the RLDS Temple." In Garr and Johnson, eds., *Missouri,* 313–35.

Smith, Joseph. *History of The Church of Jesus Christ of Latter-day Saints.* Edited by B. H. Roberts. 7 vols. 2d ed. rev. Salt Lake City: The Church of Jesus Christ of Latter-day Saints, 1932–51.

———. Letters to William W. Phelps, November 27, 1832, and January 11, 1833. Joseph Smith Collection, Church History Library, Salt Lake City.

———. *The Papers of Joseph Smith.* Edited by Dean C. Jessee. 2 vols. Salt Lake City: Deseret Book, 1989–92.

———. *Personal Writings of Joseph Smith.* Edited by Dean C. Jessee. 2d ed. Salt Lake City: Deseret Book; Provo, Utah: Brigham Young University Press, 2002.

———. *Teachings of the Prophet Joseph Smith.* Selected by Joseph Fielding Smith. Salt Lake City: Deseret Book, 1976.

Smith, Lucy Mack. *Biographical Sketches of Joseph Smith the Prophet and His Progenitors for Many Generations.* Vol. 6 of *Prominent Works in Mormon History.* Orem, Utah: Grandin Book, 1995.

Smith, William. "The Old Soldier's Testimony." *Saints' Herald,* October 4, 1884, 643–45.

Tracey, Nancy. Autobiography. Utah State Historical Society, Salt Lake City.

Wadsworth, Nelson B. *Through Camera Eyes.* Provo, Utah: Brigham Young University Press, 1975.

Welch, John W., and Erick B. Carlson, eds. *Opening the Heavens: Accounts of Divine Manifestations, 1820–1844.* Provo, Utah: Brigham Young University Press; Salt Lake City: Deseret Book, 2005.

Wells, Junius F. Letter to Joseph Fielding Smith, October 16, 1928. Church History Library, Salt Lake City.

Index

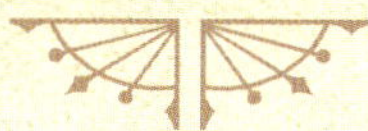

Pages on which photographs appear are designated in italic type.